How what y... to say ... at university

a guide for those who know
what they want to say
but can't find the words

Patricia Hipwell and Lyn Carter

logonliteracy

Count on **Numeracy**

First published 2016

National Library of Australia Cataloguing-in-Publication entry

Creator:	Hipwell, Patricia, author.
Title:	How to write what you want to say ... at university : a guide for those who know what they want to say but can't find the words / Patricia Hipwell and Lyn Carter; contributors, Charlotte Cottier and Jan Maskey.
ISBN:	9781925236927 (paperback)
Subjects:	Academic writing.
Other Creators/Contributors:	
	Carter, Lyn, author.
	Cottier, Charlotte.
	Maskey, Jan.
Dewey Number:	808.02

Typeset in Delicious 10 pt.

Text and cover design: **Boolarong Press**

Image of *Pencil-pusher* by Zsuzsanna Kilian

Note: Text examples of the academic writing skill have been created to demonstrate that skill. Possible inaccuracies and out-of-date information in these texts are acknowledged by the authors and do not detract from the validity of their inclusion.

Published by Boolarong Press, Salisbury, Brisbane, Australia.

Printed and bound by Watson Ferguson & Company, Salisbury, Brisbane, Australia.

contents

To Jennifer, David, John, Gareth and Elizabeth, from whom we have learned more than we have taught.

introduction

This guide, written by Lyn Carter of Count on Numeracy and Patricia Hipwell of logonliteracy, provides students at university and other tertiary institutions with the language they need to write for scholarly, or academic, purposes. It aims to provide those with limited experience in academic writing with a starting point to say what they want to say using language that academic writers use.

Most of the book is set out in a double-page format covering different forms of academic writing:

- The first page defines the purpose and things that students should know about the form of writing, and provides some relevant sentence starters.

- The second page provides useful language and an example of the skill in a short piece of writing (with the sentence starters shown in bold).

Additional sections provide more tips on improving the sophistication of writing and meeting academic expectations.

How to write what you want to say ... at university is a guide for those who know what they want to say but can't find the words. It provides a unique tool for improving writing. It suits inexperienced writers enrolled in undergraduate courses at university, including those for whom English is a second language.

This book is the fourth in a series and takes a similar approach to:

> *How to write what you want to say* by Patricia Hipwell

> *How to write what you want to say ... in mathematics* by Lyn Carter and Patricia Hipwell

> *How to write what you want to say ... in the primary years* by Catherine Black and Patricia Hipwell

Two further books are soon to be released:

> *How to write what you want to say ... in business* by Lyn Carter and Patricia Hipwell

> *How to write what you want to say ... in science* by Malcolm Carter, Lyn Carter and Patricia Hipwell

the nature of academic writing

The aim of this book is to assist university students with the process of putting their ideas on paper or on the screen in a suitable form. In many cases, the first significant contact a university teacher (lecturer or tutor) has with an undergraduate student is through writing, when the student submits work for assessment. The teacher is required to make judgements about the student based on the quality of that written work. While content is important, the negative impact of a poorly written piece of work should not be underestimated. This means that the correct presentation of written work is vital.

This book explains how to write in the forms required at university, including essays, reports of research and experiments, case studies, book and literature reviews, abstracts, and dissertations and theses. These documents usually have several sections that require various styles of writing.

Academic writing contains some common features. It

- conveys factual information, supported by evidence
- is structured, often using section headings
- uses technical language appropriate to the subject matter
- has a formal tone, avoiding features of spoken language such as overused words, contractions and clichés
- often uses passive voice
- usually has a specified word or page limit, requiring both precision and conciseness of expression
- expresses ideas positively rather than negatively
- may include illustrations and tables.

Plagiarism is a serious and reprehensible activity. Therefore, to what extent is it acceptable for students to reuse the sentence starters and useful phrases in this book in their academic writing? Plagiarism occurs when sections of text are copied and imported into one's own work with limited or no acknowledgement of the origin of the information. Even if ideas have been reworked into the student's own language, attempting to pass them off as original is also regarded as plagiarism. Students who copy anything more than a phrase without using direct quotes are copying not only someone else's ideas, but the unique way that the person expresses ideas – the author's *voice,* if you will. However, the sentence starters and useful words in this book are acceptable because they provide *ways of saying* specific to a writing skill. They are not unique to a particular writer and do not express the point of view of another writer. They are acceptable *because* of their generic nature. As students develop their writing skills and confidence, they will rely less on the reusable language in this book.

Although this book is about writing, the principles of effective writing also apply to effective spoken presentations, including seminars and conference presentations. Oral presentations require as much preparation as those in written form. Oral presentations are often preceded or followed by a written submission. So, this book will also assist with oral communication.

These ideas, and others, are developed throughout the book.

key terms and ideas defined

written product	the final text to be produced, for example, essay, report of research or an experiment, case study, book or literature review, abstract, dissertation or thesis; complex academic documents usually require the interweaving of several forms of writing
form of writing	the style of writing, for example, discussing, concluding, comparing, analysing; often several forms of writing are combined to make a written product
key task words	words used in questions to establish what is required in the answer and give a clear purpose for the type of writing required (see key task word glossary on pages 67 to 70)
purpose	the use or reason for a form of writing
things to know	important information about the form of writing
sentence starters	the opening clause of the sentence; these sentence starters are shown in bold in the examples of each form of writing; citations showing the source of the information may be added to some of these sentences
useful vocabulary	some suggested language that is characteristic of, or commonly used in, the form of writing
example	a brief example of each form of writing is provided; however, for reasons of space, the examples lack the evidence (citations and data) that are usually a feature of academic writing
modality	expressing ideas such as *probability*, *certainty*, *frequency*, and *importance* using additional words to extend the main verb
study	at university, students are required to write in many text types, often linked to the subject(s) or course being studied, for example, review, essay, experimental report, business report, legal opinion, dissertation/thesis; throughout this book, the general term *study* is used to refer to work in any or all genres
glossary	definitions of other key words used in this book (see pages 71 and 72)

analysing

purpose

examining the parts of an issue in detail and discussing or interpreting the relationship of the parts to each other and to the whole

things to know

As analysing often involves describing, comparing, explaining, interpreting and criticising, the information on those pages may also be useful.

sentence starters

… could be broken down in the following way(s): …

The issue of … can be viewed from several different perspectives.

The main similarities/differences between … and … are …

If … was/were changed, then the problem/issue/event/experiment would be affected in the following way(s): …

… would happen if … was/were changed.

… effectively combines … with …

The actions of … enable us to understand …

… was/were more than offset by …

Missing from the text is the … (view/perspective/opinion, etc.) of …

There is a complex relationship between … and …

… is a fact because …, whereas … is an opinion because …

… has increased/decreased/fluctuated over the years, causing corresponding variations in …

There is a strong correlation/connection between … and …

… is composed of/combines with …

In the case of …, the following details have emerged: …

There is very little relationship between … and …

The factors … contribute to …

In the first/second/third instance, …

    … means that …

useful vocabulary

although	differ/different	if … then …	provides
and	even if	in addition	some
and this/that	for as long as	in other respects	than
as well as	for example	in the past	thus
because	for instance	in the same way	unless
by	furthermore	is made up of	when …, then …
comprises	historically	is similar to/different from	which is/allows/gives
consists of	however	on the other hand	yet

example

Red Gum Valley Vineyards is a publicly traded winemaker located in southern Australia. It concentrates on cool-climate varietals such as pinot noir, pinot gris, and chardonnay. The company's share price **has fluctuated over the years, causing corresponding variations in** financial performance. Historically, the company tried to increase wine sales by lowering prices, leading to a slow deterioration in their financial position. There was insufficient cash flow to cover the long-term operational costs.

Three years ago, the vineyard decided to stop seeking sales at any price and increased prices to focus on gross profits. Sales fell by 20%, but **were more than offset by** an increase of 30% in gross profit. **These factors contributed to** higher net income and cash flow. Over this period, strict financial discipline reduced operating expenses by one third, helping the company's profit margins even further. These changes ensured that business stayed healthy during a difficult time for the wine industry. This is a company that has worked hard for its recent success.

[Note: a financial analysis would normally be accompanied by additional evidence such as tables and graphs.]

arguing

purpose

presenting one or both sides of an argument or case to reach a conclusion; arguing may involve the use of persuasive techniques (these are factual and logical rather than emotive) to convince others that your opinion about something is the correct one

things to know

Writing for the purpose of arguing involves having and stating a point of view or thesis. This may be written at the beginning of an extended piece. However, academic writers often weave their point of view subtly through the writing as this shows a greater degree of sophistication in writing.

Claims are often used to support the thesis. Arguments are powerful when relevant evidence and examples are used to prove the validity of the claims. Arguments are strengthened and, therefore, positions on the topic enhanced, when opposing views are refuted and disclaimed.

Opinions carry little weight without logical reasoning, examples and the inclusion of extensive research to support the arguments in the writing.

Conclusions leave the reader in no doubt about the position or point of view of the writer.

sentence starters

Nothing polarises opinion in quite the same way as the issue of ...

In recent years, opinion has become much more divided on the issue of ...

There are several arguments to support this point of view. First, consider the argument that ... — easy to state but difficult to substantiate.

The issue of ... is controversial because ...

There has been debate about ...

... has/have been opposed to ...

There are many studies that support ..., not least of which is ...

The evidence that supports this argument is accurate/credible/reliable/unreliable/difficult to substantiate because ....

While there are several arguments that support this point of view, the balance of the argument is in favour of ...

The issue of ... appears to be straightforward; however, closer inspection reveals compelling arguments both in favour of and against ...

However, to come to a conclusion, both points of view must be considered.

What is evident is that ... has been a failure.

useful vocabulary

admittedly	hence	moreover	therefore
at one level	however	nevertheless	therefore, it seems
because	if …, then …,	on the other hand	this/that
beyond doubt	in addition	one reason for	though evidence suggests
even	in conclusion	so	ultimately
first/second	inevitable/inevitably	such as	while/whilst
finally	instead	there are many reasons	without question
furthermore	likely that		

example

Nothing polarises opinion in quite the same way as the issue of "the war on drugs". This term was first coined by US President Richard Nixon in 1971 to describe a set of initiatives designed to reduce the production, distribution and consumption of illegal drugs*. While there is significant agreement that the illegal drug trade is a problem that needs to be dealt with, **there has been much debate about** how this should be achieved. **What is evident is that** the "war on drugs" strategy has been **a failure. There are several arguments to support this point of view. First**, it has been estimated that the US spends $51 billion annually in its fight against drugs*, and yet there has been no decline in the use of illegal drugs. Instead, the policy has resulted in the US having the second highest prison incarceration rate in the world, most of which is for drug-related crimes*. Moreover, by making drug use illegal rather than regulating it, the "war on drugs" has created a highly lucrative black market, increasing levels of violent crime and a marginalised, criminal underclass in American society*. Finally, the attempts to ban the consumption of alcohol in the US in the early part of the 20th century reveal that prohibition policies simply do not work – they reduce neither the use nor the abuse of drugs*. **All the evidence suggests** that it is time to start treating the use of illegal drugs as a social and health issue, rather than a criminal justice problem.

*Citation(s) providing the source(s) of this information or evidence for these assertion(s) would normally be included here.

comparing

purpose:

identifying the ways in which two or more things are similar and different

things to know

Comparing involves examining the similarities and differences between two, or among more than two, things.

A comparison is not a parallel description; that is, avoid writing about one thing and then writing about another. The best way to avoid a parallel description is to structure the text around the attributes/ qualities/properties/features of the things being compared.

sentence starters

A and B are similar in several ways, including ...

A is different from B in a number of respects.

The main difference between A and B is ...

The most striking similarity between A and B is ...

Obvious differences exist between A and B, particularly the fact that ...

This differs from ...

Researchers observed distinct/significant/major/only slight differences between A and B.

Closer inspection reveals that, while A and B appear very similar, subtle differences exist.

... and ... have more in common than ... and ..., especially the fact that ...

... and ... are similar because they both are/have ...

The similarities between A and B are insignificant when compared with their differences.

A comparison of ... and ... reveals noteworthy and significant differences.

This is similar to ...

These differences may have been critical factors in ...

The features of ... and ... are similar, whereas the features of ... and ... are different.

Initially, there were no differences between ... and ... but, as time progressed, significant differences emerged.

Just as ... is/are ..., so ... is/are ...

In so many ways, A and B are similar/comparable, and yet these are often forgotten as the differences are given prominence.

Specific differences exist between ... and ...

The similarities between ... and ... are more relevant than the differences.

Although there were similarities between ..., it may have been some key differences that ...

... are/were similar in appearance ...

useful vocabulary

alike/like/just like/ unlike	compared with	just as …, so …	on the other hand
alternative/alternatively	differs from	less/fewer than	similar in that
although	even though	likewise	similarly
among/amongst	however	more/greater than	specifically
another	in contrast	nevertheless	the way that
between	in other respects	not only … but also	whereas
both	in spite of this	one proposal	while/whilst
but	in the same way	on the contrary	
by comparison	is similar to	on the one hand	

example

Until about 30 000 years ago, Homo sapiens not only shared their habitat with Neanderthals, but also interbred with them*. **Although there were similarities between** the two "human" subspecies, **it may have been some key differences that** allowed Homo sapiens to displace their more ancient cousins*. Like humans, Neanderthals originated in Africa, but migrated to Eurasia long before humans did*. They **were similar in appearance** to modern humans, although they tended to be shorter and stockier in build and were much stronger, features that were evolutionary adaptations to the colder climate they inhabited*. Whilst they were originally perceived as being of lesser intelligence, evidence has revealed that they lived in family groups, buried their dead, made use of fire and used tools just like Homo sapiens*.

There are many hypotheses to explain why Neanderthals became extinct. One proposal is that as Homo sapiens moved out of Africa into Europe where the Neanderthals were already established, the two species came into direct competition with each other for resources, and ultimately the Neanderthals were outnumbered ten to one*. Another suggestion is that climate variation produced ecological changes to which Neanderthals, unlike modern humans, could not adapt. Their heavier bodies meant they required more energy to survive than Homo sapiens did. The Neanderthal body could run faster than a human, but only over a short distance. In contrast, Homo sapiens' body shape favoured long distance running and endurance. When food resources became scarce, **these** anatomical **differences may have been critical factors** leading to Neanderthals' extinction*.

*Citation(s) providing the source(s) of this information or evidence for these assertion(s) would normally be included here.

concluding

purpose:

drawing together the main ideas of something and restating them in a succinct way, often as a decision

things to know

A conclusion may involve the following:
- a restatement of the objective
- an overview/review/summary of what has already been said
- response to the research questions/hypotheses
- evaluation of whether experimental aims were met
- consideration of findings/conclusions in the light of existing research/theory
- your opinion (if relevant/required)
- practical implications and/or recommendations, including for the future
- limitations of the study

A conclusion NEVER introduces new information. For this reason, citations are not needed because they should have been provided when the issue was discussed earlier in the document. Allow about 10% to 15% of your word count for the conclusion.

sentence starters

A conclusion can be drawn from …

Thus, to conclude/in conclusion …

It can be concluded that …

The analysis supports the conclusion that …

The most valid conclusion is that …

In summary, …

It appears reasonable to conclude that … and, therefore, to recommend …

Therefore; it is recommended that …

Consequently, it seems better to … than …

Considering all the options, it seems better to …

An examination of the evidence shows that …

A strength of this conclusion/approach is …

The conclusions of this study/investigation are limited to …

These conclusions could also be applied/extended to …

Given that the aim of this study was to …, this report shows that this objective was partially/fully met.

The aims of the study could not be fully met because …

The following unexpected outcomes occurred: …

A further study could extend this work by …

Further studies would be required to …

useful vocabulary

accordingly	final point/finally	inconclusive/ inconclusively	significance/significant
aims	found/finding	inevitable/inevitably	so
although	goals	is/was	some doubt
applied (to)/application	hypothesis/hypotheses	limited (to)/limitation	summed (up)/ summarised/summary
because	if	much/no doubt	that/which included
clarified/clear	impact	on balance	then
concluded/conclusion	importance/important	outcome	thus
consequence/ consequently	in brief	overwhelming/ overwhelmingly	unexpected
expected	in closing	results	whether … or
extended (to)/extension			

example

In conclusion, historians and political scientists have debated whether the anti-Vietnam War movement was the catalyst that ultimately brought about the withdrawal of troops from Vietnam in 1973. **An examination of the evidence shows that** the highly visible and vocal antiwar movement reflected the war's increasing unpopularity in many Western democracies.

It has been argued that the militancy of some within the antiwar movement had an alienating effect on public opinion that diminished antiwar sentiment, and postponed the end of the war. However, this paper has demonstrated that antiwar feelings intensified during the time that militant activities increased. A legacy of this era was an escalation of cultural conflict leading to conservative backlash in later decades. **Further studies would be required to** determine if the election of conservative governments in many Western democracies in the late 70s and 80s was a regrouping of conservative forces that suffered defeat during the Vietnam War era.

contrasting

purpose

examining two or more things and focusing on the differences

things to know

Contrasting involves examining the differences between two, or among more than two, things.

Like comparing, contrasting should not result in a parallel description; that is, avoid writing about one thing and then writing about another. The best way to avoid a parallel description is to structure the text around the attributes/qualities/properties/features of the things being contrasted.

sentence starters

The main differences between ... and ... are ...

... and ... have nothing in common; only differences are apparent.

Obvious differences exist between A and B, particularly the fact that ...

This differs from ...

There are major differences of opinion about ...

... and ... are different because ... is ..., whereas ... is ...

Initially, there were no differences between ... and ... . However, as time progressed significant differences emerged.

Specific differences exist between ... and ...

The elements of ... and ... are very different.

Subtle differences exist between ... and ...

While ... is like ..., ... is like ...

Slight differences appeared at first and these became more noticeable over time.

... and ... have far less in common than would at first appear.

The distinguishing characteristics of ... make it very different from anything else.

While both ..., there are significant differences between ...

Be careful not to overlook the hidden differences between ... and ...

... and ... are not alike in any way.

A comparison of ... and ... reveals only differences.

Another major difference is the ...

By contrast, ...

There is nothing about ... and ... that is in any way similar.

This is dissimilar to ...

   is not like ... in any way.

useful vocabulary

admittedly	even though	nevertheless	other differences
alternatively	however	no commonality	rather
although	in contrast	not only ... but also	unlike
among/amongst	in no way similar	on the contrary	whereas
between	in other respects	on the one hand	while/whilst
conversely	in spite of this	on the other hand	yet
differs from	less/fewer than	opposing	
even so	more/greater than	or	

example

Phonics has long been accepted as a valid approach to teaching children to read, especially when included as part of a balanced approach to the teaching of reading*. Analytical and synthetic approaches to teaching phonics are currently used in reading development. **While both** require students to have phonological awareness (the ability to hear sounds in spoken words and discriminate between these sounds), **there are significant differences between the two approaches.** With analytical phonics, teaching begins at the whole word level and children detect phonetic patterns and are shown patterns in spelling (orthography). **By contrast**, in early teaching using synthetic phonics, children are taught a small group of the most common sounds which can be articulated together to pronounce unfamiliar words. With analytical phonics, children analyse the letter/sound patterns after the word has been identified; conversely, with synthetic phonics, the word is discovered through sounding and blending phonemes.

Another major difference is the role the alphabet plays in the two approaches. Typically, children learn the 26 letters and sounds in the analytical approach, whereas, using synthetic phonics, they are not taught the names of the letters, rather the 44 phonemes (the smallest units of sound) and their associated graphemes. Analytical phonics are taught parallel to, or sometime after, the introduction of graded or levelled readers. **This is dissimilar to** synthetic phonics, where the letter sounds are generally taught before children are introduced to books and writing. **There are major differences of opinion about** the effectiveness of the two approaches. Researchers have found that using an approach based on synthetic phonics produces slightly better results in the long term for word reading, spelling and comprehension generally*.

Citation(s) providing the source(s) of this information or evidence for these assertion(s) would normally be included here.

criticising

purpose

making judgements about something or someone, giving details to support your point of view

things to know

Academic criticism is not necessarily fault finding. Nor is it based on personal opinion. It involves making and expressing a well-reasoned judgement, based on evidence or on commonly accepted standards for scholarly work. Evaluating and analysing are closely related to criticising.
Criticising may involve drawing attention to:
- *potential areas of improvement*
- *the use of (in)appropriate methods in the research/analysis/experimentation*
- *replicability of data (can other researchers reproduce the results?)*
- *the need to consider other reasonable explanations or perspectives*
- *inconsistencies in argument or the application of logic*
- *differences in the conclusions reached by different researchers, including statements that imply certainty when doubt exists, or exaggeration of doubt when there is general agreement*
- *areas of potential conflict of interest (is the research sponsored by those with an interest in a particular outcome?)*

Academic criticism is an important part of the peer-review process.

sentence starters

This argument/approach is flawed because ...

One flaw/drawback associated with this idea is that ...

Another problem with this interpretation is that it fails to take into account ...

When evaluating ... ‹the issue›, it is necessary to ask the question ... ?

... reveals flaws in their reasoning.

A criticism of this idea is ...

The most important of these criticisms is that ...

A weakness of this approach/theory is that it fails to address the issue of ...

A criticism often levelled at this argument is that ...

A significant limitation of this explanation is ...

This argument is inconsistent with/contradicts/overlooks the widely accepted belief that ...

The problem with this argument is ...

However, such arguments tend to overlook the fact that ...

This study might have been more convincing if the author had considered ...

In this recent research/study, the author has ...

In this limited study, the author has failed to ...

These ideas have been challenged in recent years by ...

useful vocabulary

also	because	for instance	one of
and so	consequently	furthermore	therefore
another	finally	however	this
as a result	firstly	if	while/whilst
as well	for example	in addition	

example

An analysis of some of the arguments put forward by climate change deniers **reveals some flaws in their reasoning**. One of their key arguments is that the scientists who propose that humans cause global warming do not present their arguments with absolute certainty: what they write is full of terms such as "probably" and "likely". If the climate experts are not sure, argue the deniers, why should we be worried about it? **The problem with this argument is** that it reveals a lack of understanding of the fundamental nature of the scientific method of enquiry. Scientific theories are never 100% certain and are always open to reinterpretation as new evidence emerges. Probability is the language of science; there are no absolute certainties. However, 97% of climate change experts argue that the evidence strongly points towards the fact that global warming is happening and that action needs to be taken now to avoid catastrophic consequences in the future*.

Furthermore, **when evaluating the climate change denier stance, it is necessary to ask the question**: is there an underlying philosophy that shapes their views, but that has little to do with scientific evidence? For example, Roy Spencer is one of a small number of climate scientists who denies that humans are playing a significant role in global warming. He has said, "I view my job a little like a legislator, supported by the taxpayer, to protect the interests of the taxpayer and to minimize the role of government"*. This comment reveals his essentially libertarian perspective, a belief that individual choice and minimal government interference in the lives of individuals are of primary importance. As a result, such climate change deniers believe that positive action to address global warming will bring in increased government regulation, and they are opposed to such policies. **There are many other examples of** climate change deniers allowing an underlying philosophy to influence their analysis. "Scientific arguments" such as this tend to selectively quote data to support their views.

Citation(s) providing the source(s) of this information or evidence for these assertion(s) would normally be included here.

describing

purpose

giving a detailed account of the properties, qualities, features or parts of something or someone

things to know

When describing, it is not necessary to give reasons for the way things are, and a description should not include reasons 'how' or 'why'. Much academic writing begins with describing.

A concept map is a useful tool for planning a description.

Descriptions are written in the present tense if they are about something that continues to exist or an ongoing situation (present perfect tense). They use past tense if they are about something or a situation that no longer exists.

sentence starters

One of the characteristics of ... is ...

... has a number of distinguishing/special/notable features, including ...

The key features of ... are ...

... looks/sounds/feels/tastes/smells like ...

An examination of ... reveals ...

... has several distinguishing features, which include ...

The major attribute of ... is ...

... has some distinctive features/characteristics which make it unique.

... comprises/is composed of/consists of/is constructed of ...

Other important aspects include ...

The most significant elements of ... include ...

... has some very distinctive traits, especially ...

... is unlike anything else seen/experienced previously, although ...

Upon examination, it is seen that ...

There is significant ...

The most obvious feature of ... is ...

Most prominent is ...

Other less important features are ...

Important though ... is, it is not the most relevant factor in the description.

additionally	as well as	in addition	shows
all	besides	include	some/sometimes
along with	combines	is composed of	such as
also	extra	mainly	the following characteristics
although	extra features	moreover	too
and	for example	not only ... but also	
apart from	furthermore	rather than	
as shown in/by	however	several	

example

One of the world's truly awe-inspiring natural features is the Grand Canyon, located in Northern Arizona. It is estimated to be between five and six million years old. The Grand Canyon **has a number of distinguishing features, the most prominent of which is** the layered rock. The Canyon walls **are composed of** nearly 40 rock layers. This phenomenon has allowed geologists to study the progression of geological processes in the area.

In addition to the spectacular cliffs, the Colorado River snakes its way through the Grand Canyon. It has carved a deep, narrow gorge, which is nearly 2 kilometres deep in many places. The dry climate prevents the gorge from widening and this further contributes to the spectacular appearance of the Grand Canyon.

Another distinctive feature, which makes the Canyon **unique,** is the presence of a diversity of ecosystems and habitats. Only the Alpine tundra is absent. At higher elevations, the slopes support vegetation such as ponderosa and pinyon pines, sagebrush scrub, pinyon-juniper woodlands and blackbrush. South-facing slopes, which receive plenty of sun, support desert vegetation.

There is significant variation in temperatures throughout the Canyon during the day and throughout the year. Temperatures on the North and South Rim are generally much cooler than those in the Inner Canyon. Visitors should prepare for these differences and also sudden weather changes that can occur, especially in the autumn.

discussing

purpose

considering the results of research and the implications of those results; considering both sides of an issue about something, without necessarily coming to a conclusion

things to know

Discussing is often thought to be associated with spoken language rather than writing. In academic writing, it is a written debate where you are using your reasoning skills, backed up by evidence, to make a case for and against something, or to consider the advantages and disadvantages of something. A discussion should include a conclusion.

In science, a discussion analyses and interprets the results of an experiment.

Past tense is used to discuss facts, results, outcomes and past events, but present tense is used to describe theory, conclusions and propositions.

sentence starters

Several aspects of the issue need to be discussed, especially …

The factors that contribute to this situation include …

If the topic is placed under the microscope, then it becomes clear that …

A cursory exploration of this issue suggests some hidden complexities, including …

In addition to what is visible, there are other aspects worthy of discussion.

There are several aspects to the problem to be examined, particularly …

The overall purpose of this study was to determine …

The results of this investigation revealed/indicated/showed that …

This trend is/was shown most clearly in …

Another important finding was that …

The most interesting/thought-provoking finding from the study was that …

A more detailed analysis of the data reveals some interesting trends viz. …

It is interesting to note that …

One unanticipated/unexpected finding was that …

Contrary to expectations, the study revealed …

The results of this study supported/corroborated/were consistent with earlier findings that showed …

The findings of the current study do not support previous research in the field.

Some researchers have speculated that …

The issue that emerges/emerged from this data is/was …

Several questions remain unanswered and could be the focus of further research.

useful vocabulary

also	as a result	furthermore	therefore
although	because	however	this
and	clearly	if	thus
another	for example/instance	in addition	which means that

example

According to the Population Clock published online by the Australian Bureau of Statistics (ABS)*, the nation's population reached 24 million on 16 February 2016. **A more detailed analysis of the ABS population data* reveals some interesting trends** that will no doubt have long-term implications for government planning and social policy. For example, the current fertility rate (births per woman) is 1.8 (below the replacement rate), compared with 2.9 in 1968, which means that Australia's population will continue to be an aging one. **This trend is shown most clearly in** the data for median age (the age at which half the population is older and half the population is younger). In 1901 Australia's median age was 22.5; this rose to 27.8 in 1968. However, by 2015 the median age had increased to 37.4. This significant rise in the median age over the last 50 years is closely linked to improvements in life expectancy, and also because there has not been a war in which many people died. For instance, the data reveals that life expectancy for Australian women has risen from 58.8 years in 1901 to 84.4 years in 2014. **The issue that emerges from this data is** how Australia will deal with an aging population in the future where, if current trends continue, a shrinking workforce and the lower tax revenue it provides will be required to support a growing elderly population.

Citation(s) providing the source(s) of this information or evidence for these assertion(s) would normally be included here.

17

elaborating

purpose

giving more information or detail about something

things to know

Elaborating is not "waffle" or repetition or writing to increase word length. When elaborating, the writer should go into greater depth about the topic by including more details. The inclusion of relevant examples is a way to elaborate; so too is the inclusion of evidence (supported by relevant quotes).

The inclusion of definitions and relevant examples (supported by quotes or citations) are ways to elaborate.

sentence starters

Close/careful scrutiny/observation reveals …

A detailed examination shows …

The meaning of … has changed over time.

The information is accurate and supported by evidence, especially …

… supports the interpretation of the facts, which is …

… attests to the relevancy of the information.

Under these circumstances, … would apply.

One interpretation of the findings could be …

This had a significant social/cultural/economic/political/scientific impact because …

For example, consider the phenomenon of ….

There is more to the topic/issue than at first appears; therefore, it should be looked at deeply.

At a glance, it is clear that …; however, a more detailed analysis of … reveals …

One interpretation could be …

Looking more closely, it is apparent that …

There are more details to be examined and these include …

In addition to what is visible, there are other aspects worthy of discussion.

The diagram provides additional information, especially as it shows …

There developed/emerged a growing emphasis on …

A further development/innovation was …

useful vocabulary

additionally/in addition	besides	given this fact	reveals
albeit	certainly	however	specifically
also	clearly	if ... then	such as
and	closely	in order to	supports
and so	especially	indicates	thus
and this	for example/instance	interprets	under these circumstances
apparently	for this reason	it becomes clear	when
as revealed by	from this	it is clear	
	furthermore	moreover	

example

At a glance, it is clear that in the 21st century we are a world of ever more voracious consumers; however, a more detailed analysis of the sociology of consumerism reveals a fascinating insight into how our attitudes towards consumption have changed over time. Certainly, modern economies rely extensively on people consuming more and more. For example, consider the phenomenon of the Boxing Day sales: Christmas Day is spent unwrapping "stuff" given by other people, and then the following day people head out to stores to participate in a shopping frenzy to buy yet more "stuff".

The very meaning of the word consumption has changed over time. When it first entered English usage in the 13th century, it meant "to exhaust and use up something". However, by the 17th century it developed a more positive connotation, and consumption came to be seen as something valuable that produced improvements in people's lives, shaped their identities and advanced society*. Although people have always consumed, in Ming China and Renaissance Italy in the 15th and 16th centuries there developed a growing emphasis on acquiring personal possessions with the aim of creating comfort in the home. By the 19th century, shopping emerged as a distinct social activity, with its emphasis on acquiring new things, and this was fuelled by the Industrial Revolution and its focus on the mass production of goods. A further innovation was the modern department store, with its emphasis on displaying goods for sale. This had a significant cultural impact, with consuming becoming a recreational activity: people now "go shopping" rather than "do shopping"*.

Today, shoppers are confronted by a seemingly endless supply of goods, and are constantly urged by advertisers to upgrade and update, yet fundamental changes in consumption patterns are needed. In order to have environmentally sustainable consumption in the future, more ethical and responsible consumption decisions may be needed.

*Citation(s) providing the source(s) of this information or evidence for these assertion(s) would normally be included here.

evaluating

purpose

considering something or someone to make a judgement of value or worth

things to know

Evaluations are usually supported by evidence.

A thorough evaluation examines reasons for and against a proposal or point of view, such as relevant advantages (pros) and disadvantages (cons) of something.

sentence starters

... is a more suitable or viable choice/option/solution because ...

Despite the criticism of ..., it is a viable alternative.

... is better/more effective/more appealing/more enjoyable than ...

... evokes a feeling of ... on the one hand, mixed with feelings of ... on the other.

An examination of the options reveals that ...

If ... is compared with ..., several differences emerge and these include ...

There are significant advantages/disadvantages of ...

To improve the effectiveness of ..., several changes need to be made, which include ...

The appeal of ... lies in ...

The worst feature of ... is ..., because ...

... is well worth considering; however, ...

The following criteria will be used to evaluate the idea/proposal/scheme/product: ...

The most outstanding performance was by ..., as he/she/they ...

Even though parts of ... are weak, the overall effect is ...

There are several flaws in the argument and these include ...

... is more suitable/logical/ethical/appropriate than ...

... can be considered to be [another] disadvantage.

Some would argue/have argued that ...

There are strengths, on the one hand, and significant flaws on the other.

It worked reasonably well when ...; however, ... was especially effective.

useful vocabulary

albeit	effective/ineffective	in other respects	therefore
although	especially	in particular	thus
apart from	for example	in spite of this	when ... then ...
because of this	furthermore	less/fewer	whereas
better/worse	greater/more	nevertheless	while/whilst
by comparison	hence	on the other hand	with regard to
by contrast	however	regardless	
despite this/the fact that	if ... then ...	the effect of	

example

The decision to take a break (commonly known as a "gap year") between school and tertiary study, or at some point during that study, is one that many students are taking. **The appeal of** taking a year or two (gap "years" can be longer than a single year) away from study **lies in** the fact that it provides many opportunities. The experience gained during the gap year can prepare students for university both academically and socially. However, unless the year is planned, it may be spent rather purposelessly. **Some have argued that** the gap year is the longest "holiday" a person experiences in their lifetime*. It follows that serious thought should be given to the decision. **There are significant disadvantages of** taking a gap year. Travel is expensive and a gap year can leave students short of money. On the other hand, there are many opportunities to earn money and this can alleviate the financial pressures associated with university education. Taking a gap year **is worth considering as** an opportunity to gain new skills or to try some career options, including voluntary work. Students may take part of the year to prepare themselves for their courses by reading and gaining relevant work experience in their chosen field. Students will be "out of sync" with school friends who have gone straight to university from school and **this can be considered to be another disadvantage**. Furthermore, students may lose their university places, especially if they do not make their decision to defer clear to the university. Taking a gap year **is a viable option**; however, students should carefully evaluate the pros and cons before making a decision.

Citation(s) providing the source(s) of this information or evidence for these assertion(s) would normally be included here.

explaining

purpose

making something understandable by giving a detailed account of its properties, qualities, features or parts, how it works, and why it is as it is

things to know

An explanation includes the 'what' (description), 'how' (process) and 'why' (justification or cause and effect).

The information elsewhere in this book about descriptions and justifications may also be useful when explaining.

Many writers confuse the words affect (verb) and effect (noun). Make sure you understand their usage.

sentence starters

... is the name given to ...

There are several aspects to this issue, especially ...

The process of ... is caused by ...

They are most likely to occur where/when ...

... works by ...

There are several reasons for ...

... has several causes including ...

It is also likely to cause ...

The factors that contribute to this situation include ...

The main effect of ... is ...

... will also affect ...

As a result of ... several unforeseen events have occurred, including ...

The current situation exists because ...

... are usually caused when/by ...

The main reason that ... occurs is ...

Other factors that contribute to this phenomenon include ...

The reason for this situation is not clear; however, ...

... can lead to ...

This has had an impact on ... and consequently ...

This has happened because ...

If ... were to change, then ... would happen.

This event happens rarely/frequently/occasionally/on a regular basis because ...

affect	for this reason	occurs when/where	that is caused by
also	from this/these/that	phenomenon	the effect of
and so	generally	process	the reason for
and this leads to	hence	provided that	then
because	how	resulting in	therefore
caused/causation	if ... then ...	results (from)/result (of)	thus
consequently	is called	since	unless
contributed to	it follows that	so	what
due to	known as	so that	when ... then ...
factors	led to		why

example

In the past 200 years, the world has been warming. **This process of** global warming **is caused by** a natural phenomenon called the greenhouse effect.

The Earth's climate is driven by a continuous flow of energy, including heat, from the sun. During the day, the heat from the sun passes through the Earth's atmosphere and warms the Earth's surface. As the surface temperature rises, the heat energy radiates back into the atmosphere. Some of this heat is absorbed by a naturally occurring layer of atmospheric gases such as carbon dioxide, water vapour, methane, nitrous oxide, ozone and halocarbons, often called greenhouse gases. This layer acts as a blanket trapping the heat. It shields the earth from the cold of the universe, particularly at night when there is no sun.

If the quantity of greenhouse gases in the atmosphere increases, then the layer gets thicker, acting like an extra blanket warming the earth. Prolonged global warming can lead to rising land temperatures causing longer droughts, more bush fires, and a spread in tropical diseases. **It is also likely to cause** increased ocean temperatures causing glaciers and polar ice caps to melt, rises in sea levels, more cyclones and flooding, and changes in ocean currents. Increased temperatures will also affect the survival of plants and animals, on land and in the sea. The higher temperatures will favour some organisms and cause others to change their behaviour or die out.

Citations providing evidence for the many assertions in this example would normally be included.

generalising

purpose

developing a broad statement, based on evidence, that seems to be true in most situations or for most people

things to know

Although a general statement is based on evidence, it does not include details such as data, quotations, or examples.

In some circumstances, generalising can also be called theorising or inductive reasoning.

Generalisations may be supported by a diagram or model that shows the connections between the important ideas.

sentence starters

In the usual course of events, …

In the majority of cases, …

While there are exceptions to the rule, for the most part … applies.

A number of general statements can be made about …

There are exceptions to this general trend although, for the most part, … is relevant/evident/significant.

Generally speaking, … is relevant in this case.

In this instance, the general rule of … is significant.

To summarise, then, the following generalisations are apparent: …

Although some anomalies exist, a general pattern emerges …

The study found that, although …, a pattern was evident.

… is more usual than …

An examination of the data reveals several generalisations …

From the evidence, it is possible to suggest the following generalisation(s): …

More general trends appear in the longer rather than the shorter term.

For the most part, …

The general characteristics of … are …

The principle of … can be applied to …

… is a broad statement which encompasses the essential elements of …

In a more general way, the ideas can be represented like this: …

… has the same general idea as …

… fits the general pattern of …

useful vocabulary

as likely as not	in most/a large number of cases	mostly	regularly
assumed/assumption	in the main	normally	suggested
broadly speaking	it seems that	often	supported
centrally	likely	on average	theory
characteristically	mainly	on the whole	therefore
commonly	many	pattern	typically
essentially	more likely than not	primarily	usually
generally/general	more often than not	proposition	widespread
if so	most	quintessential/ quintessentially	
in common	most often	reasonably	

example

This study found that, although there were multiple interpretations of *numeracy* amongst teachers, **a pattern was evident. For the most part,** mathematics teachers considered that numeracy is developed outside the mathematics classroom since that is where life-related contexts arise naturally. Teachers in other learning areas typically held that numeracy is part of mathematics since that is where the skills and content are first taught. **In the majority of cases,** teachers did not view numeracy in the four dimensions of mathematical knowledge, tools, contexts and dispositions. The multiple interpretations of numeracy amongst teachers led to a general breakdown in communications within the schools and confusion in administrative practices, policy development, and leadership. It resulted in a widespread lack of clarity about the responsibility for numeracy in each of the schools studied. It seems that a significant barrier to the successful embedding of numeracy in all learning areas is the multiple interpretations of numeracy amongst teachers, especially if they are unaware that their colleagues may have different understandings. If so, the first step for successfully embedding numeracy across the entire school curriculum is the development of a shared understanding of numeracy amongst all teachers.

inferring

purpose

using what is provided to make meaning or arrive at an answer, to uncover the answer even though it is not directly said or stated

things to know

Inference involves combining what you see (in words, tables or visual images) with what you know to generate meaning or understanding. It follows that inferences based on the same set of facts may vary from one person to another if their knowledge of the situation is different. Valid inferences can be adequately supported by the information in the text, whereas invalid inferences cannot be supported by the information in the text.

sentence starters

It can/could be inferred that …

It means that …

As a result, …

It is unclear what … means, but a plausible explanation is …

It is reasonable to assume that …

Reading between the lines suggests that …

My interpretation of … is supported by …

While … is commonly understood to mean …, I think it means …

There are several interpretations of the same event, but the most popular is …

The answer to the question is not obvious, but I think …

The texts say, "…" and this means, …

This interpretation is supported by the following evidence: …

… reveals a great deal about the character/situation/problem/topic.

It is likely that … because …

This may suggest that …

The illustration supports the information in the text by …

Smith (2008) stated … and this directly supports the findings of Jones (2010), who noted …

The graph/table shows … and this could mean …

The data reveals the following trends: …

Even though it is not directly stated, it is apparent that …

A common but incorrect interpretation is …

… has several possible interpretations; however, … is the most likely.

useful vocabulary

although	despite	interpreted/ interpretation	reveal
and	due to	it appears	revealed by
as a result	even though	it is clear	since
because	evidently	it is evident	the reason for
by contrast	far from it	it seems	therefore
can be inferred	hence	may mean that	this is how
clearly	however	might mean	this is why
concluded (that)	in other words	results	whereas
consequently			

example

Age group	% in 2011	% in 2012
12–17	76	81
18–24	80	80
25–34	68	68
35–44	63	65
45–54	45	55
55–64	31	34
Above 65	15	23

Source: http://www.convinceandconvert.com/social-media-research/11-shocking-new-social-media-statistics-in-america/

The table shows the growth between 2011 and 2012 in the percentage of Americans who had a personal profile page on any social networking website. **This data reveals** that, across all age groups, the percentage of people participating in social networking either remained steady or increased. The highest participation rates occurred in the 12–24 age groups. **A possible interpretation** of this fact is that people in these age groups are digital natives. In other words, they were born during or after the advent of the digital age. **As a result**, they have grown up with technology and feel comfortable with it. **It also suggests the** importance of social networking to young people. It is clearly one of the main ways in which they communicate with each other. Interestingly, the 45–54 age group saw the greatest increase in usage. **This may suggest that** people in this group have become digital immigrants: they were born before the existence of digital technology, but have increasingly taken up the use of it in later life. **It could be inferred that** this is because they have been exposed to more technology in the workplace. By contrast, the over 65 age group, many of whom are retired, remain limited users of social networking.

interpreting

purpose
examining a piece of text and explaining its meaning or significance, often from a particular point of view

things to know
Texts can be interpreted in many ways. As with inferring, interpreting requires combining what you see (in words, tables or visual images) with what you know to generate meaning or understanding. Prior knowledge and experience provide the lens through which information can be interpreted, therefore multiple interpretations of the same information or data are possible.

sentence starters

While it is unclear what this statement means, one reasonable interpretation is that …

It is reasonable to assume that …

The text states … and this means …

Most experts/historians/scholars agree that …

Scholars have argued that …

This interpretation of … is supported by …

There are several interpretations of …, but the most common one is …

A more radical interpretation is that …

This interpretation differs from/contrasts with that of …, who argues that …

This interpretation ignores much of the research that has been conducted in …

This interpretation is supported by the following evidence: …

It is likely that … because …

A careful analysis of … reveals a great deal about …

It is especially significant for the insight it provides into …

This text provides a valuable insight into …

A common but incorrect interpretation is that …

… can be examined from the point of view of …

This could mean that …

These results must be interpreted/used with caution because …

… can be viewed as …

useful vocabulary

after	clearly	it appears	might mean
as a result	evidently	it is clear	revealed by
as such	however	it is evident	since
at the same time	for example	it is unclear	such
because	in other words	it seems	
but	in particular	may mean	

example

The *Res Gestae Divi Augusti* (The Deeds of the Divine Augustus)* was written by the first Roman Emperor Augustus, giving an account of his life and achievements. After his death, many copies of the text were made and carved on stone pillars, which were erected throughout the vast Roman Empire. **Scholars have argued that**, in the ancient world before the invention of printing, such inscriptions **can be viewed as** a form of political propaganda, presenting the principate (the new form of government in Rome that Augustus established at the end of the civil war) in a positive light*. As such, it is a rare first person account from an ancient ruler, but this also means **it must be used with caution** when trying to compile a comprehensive and balanced picture of what motivated Augustus. At the same time, **the *Res Gestae* is especially significant for the insight it provides into** how Augustus wanted to be viewed by the Roman people. For example, the inscription records the political offices and honours that he held, but he also seems to go to great lengths to emphasise the numerous offices he refused to take and the privileges he refused to accept. He wrote: "I surpassed all others in influence, yet my official powers were no greater than those of my colleagues in office."* **Most historians agree* that** this desire to present himself as a first among equals is consistent with a ruler who, from the beginning, wanted to portray himself as "restoring" the old Roman Republic and its traditions. However, Augustus had grabbed power through force and clever manipulation of the political situation, and the principate he subsequently established was essentially an absolute monarchy. **It is likely that** Augustus was very conscious of the traditional Roman dislike for kingship (the expulsion of the last Roman king had occurred 500 years earlier) and so desired to present his reign in a different light.

Citation(s) providing the source(s) of this information or evidence for these assertion(s) would normally be included here.

introducing

purpose

starting a text by describing what it is about

things to know

Introductions can include the aims/objectives of the document, why the topic matters, key definitions, important issues, a summary of the methods to be used, and an outline of the structure of the document.

The section on transitioning on pages 48 and 49 includes information that can assist in writing introductions.

sentence starters

It has been suggested that ...

A common view is that ...

There are two main views about ...

It was hypothesised that ...

The background to this issue was ...

This study/investigation/experiment was ...

This study aimed to ...

The aim of this study/investigation/experiment was ...

The method used to explore this issue was ...

The issue is/was important because ...

The investigation/experiment is interesting/significant/useful because ...

The theory relevant to this investigation/experiment is ...

Research suggests that ...

Before continuing, it is necessary to explain the meaning of some key terms.

The important concepts in this study/investigation/experiment were ...

This essay/article/paper/report/thesis contains ... sections, as follows: ...

An outline of this essay/article/paper/report/thesis is as follows: ...

... is defined as ...

aim/aimed	find/finding	involved	purpose
any	following	is in the third section	relationship
between	for example	issues	significant/significance
comprised	for instance	mattered/matters	such as
commonly	goal	meant (that)/meaning	the final section
connection	if any	method	the next section
defined/definition	important/importance	methodology	the reason for
determine	included	objective	this section
essential	intended/intention	on the one hand	was defined as
examined	investigated	on the other hand	was made up of
explored			

example

It has been suggested that steel is the most important metal in the world because it is the most widely used*. Steel is an essential part of the construction of buildings, motor vehicles, appliances and infrastructure such as roads and railways. Most large modern structures, such as stadiums, skyscrapers, bridges and airports, are supported by a steel skeleton. Even those made of concrete use steel for reinforcing. It is essential that steel is able to withstand corrosion.

The aim of this experiment was twofold: (a) to determine the conditions that promote the corrosion of steel; and (b) to find how corrosion can be prevented or reduced.

The important concepts in this experiment were steel and corrosion. Steels are alloys of iron (Fe) and other elements, primarily carbon (C), widely used because of their high tensile strengths and low costs. Corrosion **is defined as** a natural process, involving the destruction of materials (usually metals or alloys) by the surrounding environment through chemical and electrochemical changes*. In the case of iron and steel, corrosion is commonly called rusting.

This experimental **report contains five sections**. Following this introduction, some background research is presented, leading to the development of six hypotheses about the rusting of steel. The second section on experimental process describes the experimental design, procedures, and method, and is followed by a third section that presents the observed data. In the discussion section, the data is analysed and deductions are made. The report ends with recommendations to prevent the corrosion of steel and a conclusion.

Citation(s) providing the source(s) of this information or evidence for these assertion(s) would normally be included here.

justifying

purpose

showing or proving that a decision, action or idea about something is reasonable or necessary by giving sound, logical and appropriate reasons for it

things to know

A complete justification describes the decision and then provides the reasons for that decision. It answers the question 'why?'.

It explains why you support a course of action or have a particular point of view.

sentence starters

There are several/many reasons for this recommendation/recommended action/decision, including …

The weight of evidence would suggest that …

On balance, the evidence supports the view/opinion/decision that …

Consequently, it would seem better to … because …

… is a valid recommendation/suggestion based on …

… is a better option because …

… will prove to be the best decision in the long term because …

The reasons that support the choice of … are based on factual evidence.

… is a good idea because …

The best decision is … because …

… is a reasonable/necessary action because …

… shows an intelligent response to the problem/issue/topic of …

Circumstances suggest the following course of action because …

… is well supported by the evidence, which states that …

The decision to … is an effective response to changing circumstances.

For now, … is the better choice of options because …

useful vocabulary

acted/action	correct	likely	situation
adds weight to	decision	logic/logical/logically	substantiated
assumed	demonstrated/ demonstration	plausible	supported
although	explain(s) why	produces	therefore
because	find	proposition	using
calculated/calculations	hence	proved/proof	validated
confirmed/confirms	however	reasons/reasonable/ reasoning	verified
consequently	justified/justification	similarly	why

example

The rusting wrecks of ships sunk during World War II create a high risk of serious environmental damage. Action to prevent leakages of dangerous substances carried by the ships must be urgently investigated. **There are several reasons for** this recommended action.

During World War II, 1554 ships were sunk*. All of these vessels contained fuel, and many carried explosives and toxic cargoes. They have now been in a corrosive environment for more than 70 years. It is likely that corrosion will release these dangerous and polluting substances into the marine environment.

The cost of environmental damage through uncontrolled leakage of these dangerous substances and pollutants will be high. It is likely to outweigh the cost of locating the wrecks and either sealing them to prevent leakages or removing the dangerous substances*.

Action is needed at both an international and a local level. Given the global nature of the problem, the United Nations should be the body to coordinate the action.

*Citation(s) providing the source(s) of this information or evidence for these assertion(s) would normally be included here.

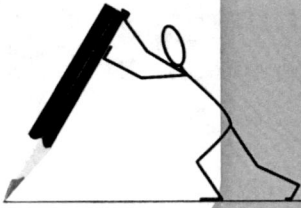

providing evidence

purpose

referring to sources, data, illustrations and other evidence about something to support the points that have been made

things to know

An important method of providing evidence is the inclusion of supporting citations and references. For more detail on citations and references, see the presentation section on pages 56 to 58.

Quotations are one way of providing evidence. More details of how to use quotations are on the next page.

sentence starters

Analysis of the data suggests ...

The evidence reveals ...

The graph shows that ...

It is clear from the table that ...

According to the figures in Table A, ...

As shown by the information in ...,

Clear trends are evident between ‹date› and ‹date› and these are ...

If the trend continues, then by ‹date› it is projected that ...

As seen in Figure A, ...

A survey of ... found that ...

Compared with the data in Table A, the data in Table B shows ...

... can be supported by the information in Figure A.

According to ‹Author› (‹date›), who stated that ...,

‹Author› (‹date›) argued that ... and this is supported by ‹Author› (‹date›).

The evidence collected allows the following observations to be made: ...

The evidence is convincing because it is stated so clearly.

useful vocabulary

according to	closely	illustrates	less/more than
almost	confirmed by	in addition to	refutes
also	contradicts	in detail	reveals
approximately	evident/evidently	indeed	shows
as well as	for example	indicates	such as
based on	for instance	it is clear that	suggest/suggests
case in point	for this reason	means	support/supports
clearly	furthermore	moreover	thorough

example

A survey of nearly 8000 Australian teachers **found that** approximately half of them undertook NAPLAN test preparation at least three times in the fortnight before the tests, with a further third practising more than six times with their students (Dulfer, Polesel, & Rice, 2012).

> citation

Almost half of the teachers advised that they undertook some form of NAPLAN practice at least weekly in the five months before the tests. Approximately 80% of teachers agreed that they had prepared students

> data

by teaching to the test and that their teaching practice had changed to emphasise the areas assessed by NAPLAN testing. Almost 23% of secondary teachers did not undertake any preparation for NAPLAN testing with their students. According to the same survey, more than 80% of teachers stated that NAPLAN preparation was adding to an already crowded curriculum, whilst 59% believed that NAPLAN was affecting the range of teaching strategies they used. A further three quarters of teachers believed that NAPLAN was having an impact on the way in which schools viewed the curriculum, with literacy and numeracy elevated in importance. The study concluded that "it seems likely, therefore, that through regular test practice, or a focus on specific skills

> quote

needed for the NAPLAN, the tests may be impacting on the breadth of curriculum that Australian student's [sic] experience" (Dulfer et al., 2012, p. 27).

quoting

purpose

using the exact words of the author (direct quotations) as evidence in writing

things to know

While it is useful to use the original words of the author when they carry special significance, direct quoting should not be the primary strategy for presenting evidence in your writing.

Text that has been directly quoted (reproduced word-for-word) from another source should be clearly marked, by the use of double quotation marks if fewer than 40 words (for example "quoted text"), or an indented block without quotation marks in the case of longer quotations.

Quotes should be reproduced exactly as in the original. Ellipsis (...) points in the middle of a quote show that some words have been omitted. If extra word(s) are needed for the quote to make sense they should be inserted in square brackets. If the quote contains a spelling or grammatical error, it should not be corrected, but [sic] can be inserted to show that it was written that way in the original quote (see the example on page 35). Single quotation marks are used for a quote within a quote.

The source, date and page number of the quotation should be cited immediately after the quotation (if quoting from an unnumbered web page or document, give the title of the page or section heading and the paragraph number). There are several methods of citing the source of a quotation. Most faculties have a preferred citation/reference style as each discipline tends to use only one or two styles. If in doubt, check with the faculty or a teacher about the preferred style. For more detail see the presentation section on pages 56 to 58.

sentence starters

According to ...

In a speech presented to ... on ...

... argued/declared/was adamant that ...

He/she asserted that/strongly argued that ...

In his/her publication/report, dated ..., ... presented the argument that ...

In this article/book/paper, ... queries/challenges/repudiates/demolishes the argument that ...

Clearly the author in ‹name of document› is attempting to position the reader to believe that ...

This argument is representative of a commonly held view at the time which was/that ...

...'s argument exemplifies the orthodox interpretation that ...

This article/book/paper corroborates/reaffirms/is consistent with the argument that ...

Although this evidence speaks loudly about ..., it should be treated with caution, considering that ...

The evidence presented in this article/book/paper suggests ...

useful vocabulary

according to	contradicted	in addition	quotation/quote
also	for example	instead	resulting
as well as	for instance	it is clear that	shows
clearly	furthermore	moreover	such

See also the alternatives to said section on page 65.

example

> ... it must be <u>a peace without victory</u>. It is not pleasant to say this. I beg that I may be permitted to put my own interpretation upon it and that it may be understood that no other interpretation was in my thought. I am seeking only to face realities and to face them without soft concealments. Victory would mean peace forced upon the loser, <u>a victor's terms imposed upon the vanquished</u>. It would be <u>accepted in humiliation, under duress,</u> at an intolerable sacrifice, and <u>would leave a sting, a resentment, a bitter memory</u> upon which terms of peace would rest, not permanently, but only as upon quicksand. <u>Only a peace between equals can last</u>, only a peace the very principle of which is equality and a common participation in a common benefit. The right state of mind, the right feeling between nations, is as necessary for <u>a lasting peace</u> as is the just settlement of vexed questions of territory or of racial and national allegiance.

Take a block quotation, select the key phrases you wish to quote, weave them into your sentences and then add the citations, showing the source and page number(s) of the quote(s).

> **In a speech presented to the US Senate on 22 January 1917,** a little more than two months before the US joined its allies to fight in World War One, President Woodrow Wilson was already contemplating the nature of the post-war peace settlement. **He was adamant that** for "a lasting peace" to be created, it would be necessary to depart from the traditional method where "a victor's terms [were] imposed upon the vanquished" (p. ...). The problem with such traditional peace conditions, **Wilson argued**, was that for the loser it was "accepted in humiliation, under duress ... and would leave a sting, a resentment, a bitter memory" (p. ...). The resulting settlement would not bring lasting peace, but would falter and fail because it rested as if "upon quicksand". Instead, **Wilson declared that** "only a peace between equals can last": he was setting the future peacemakers the difficult task of trying to achieve "a peace without victory" (p. ...).

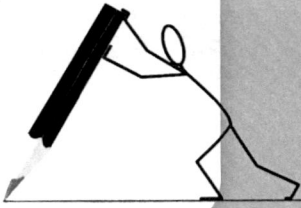

recommending

purpose

suggesting a course of action for consideration by others; providing reasons (usually the findings of research or investigation) in favour of the suggestion

things to know

Recommendations are an important part of some forms of writing, for example, reports of research, business activity and legal opinions.

sentence starters

Therefore, it is recommended that …

It appears reasonable to conclude that …, and therefore to recommend …

In spite of …, the best solution is …

Based on the findings, the following recommendations are put forward for discussion: …

There are too many problems associated with; … therefore, … is recommended.

My recommendation, after looking at all the evidence, is …

The following recommendations, listed in order of priority, are put forward for consideration: …

Based on the analysis of the situation, the following recommendations have emerged: …

I recommend the following changes: …

For the future, it is recommended that …

In light of the problem of …, a suitable solution would include …

To achieve its goals, the organisation needs to …

The sensible option is to …

A further proposal is to …

The following recommendation should be enacted as soon as possible: …

A list of the proposed recommendations with a summary of the reasons for each follows: …

In the light of all available data, the proposed recommendation is …

There are a couple of recommendations from which to choose.

A strength of this approach would be …

There are no guarantees that these recommendations will work; however, to do nothing may see the situation worsen.

useful vocabulary

accordingly	general	is favoured	these include
additionally	hence	is recommended	thus
all things considered	however	is valid	to act upon
as a result	if … then …	moreover	to conclude
because	in summary	on balance	to summarise then
consequently	in the end	so	we can conclude
could/should/would	in the final instance	then	we can recommend
finally	is desirable	therefore	will achieve

example

This study has demonstrated that teen crime is a problem with a long history, and has argued that it would be impossible to eliminate. However, it can be reduced with time, money, and a combined effort from governments, community groups and individuals. **Therefore, it is recommended that** free, after-school programs be provided. For example, sport, art, music, and drama activities, as well as interesting volunteer activities in the community, would help engage teenagers in meaningful activities outside school. More part-time jobs for young people, supported by state and local programs, would provide a source of income for them (reducing the incentive for theft) as well as productive work for the community. **A further proposal is to** assist families through schools and community organisations in promoting family closeness to support teenagers at the family level. **A strength of this approach would be** an increase in productive teenage behaviour and safer streets and neighbourhoods for the community.

reflecting

purpose

responding in a personal way to experiences, situations, events or new information by making personal connections with the new material

things to know

Use of the personal pronouns 'I', 'me' and 'my' is acceptable in reflective writing because personal responses are encouraged and respected.

Language choices may be more informal than with other forms of academic writing.

sentence starters

Previously I thought/did not think that …

This is similar to/different from …

My previous experience(s) with … led me to …

For me the most meaningful/significant/important/relevant/useful aspect(s)/element(s)/experience(s)/issue(s)/idea(s) was (were) …

Important learning occurred when …

Significant understandings developed from …

It was likely/unlikely, then, that …

From the outset …

The valuable learning that I took from this experience was …

However, when the …

Because I was responsible for …

We achieved a successful outcome because …

This knowledge/understanding/skill is important to me as a learner because …

… has challenged/confirmed/affirmed my understandings/beliefs about …

… has had a profound/significant/enduring/unsettling/disquieting effect on my understandings of …

It is unlikely that I will view … in this way again.

I am still uncertain about …

I will incorporate … into my thinking and practice.

   Now I realise …

additionally	because of	initially	previously
alternatively	elements	makes me	relevant
aspects	experience	meaningful	significant
at first	furthermore	means that	subsequently
at the time	important	might be	useful

example

For our last philosophy assignment, we were required to work in groups of three. The assessment criteria specified that the assignment be broken into parts and shared among group members. **My previous experience with** group assignments **led me to** approach this one with little enthusiasm. **From the outset**, we could not agree on how to divide the work, with all members complaining that they had more to do than the others did. Cooperation between group members was at risk because of this perceived unfairness. **It was unlikely, then, that** my group would attain the higher achievement that results from cooperative learning experiences, as identified by researchers in this field*. Our interdependence was not positive. **However, when the** group thought less about the amount of work and more about our individual strengths, we found allocating the parts of the assignment much easier to do. **Because I was responsible for** aspects of the assignment where my natural strengths lay, I no longer perceived the amount of work as an issue; neither did the other group members. **The valuable learning that I took from this experience was** that arguing about who is doing more work is petty and counterproductive. **We achieved a successful outcome because** we activated and built on each other's strengths.

*Citation(s) providing the source(s) of this information or evidence for these assertion(s) would normally be included here.

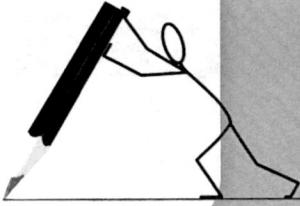

reviewing
academic literature

purpose

providing a critical overview of the academic debate about a topic (called a literature review)

things to know

In an academic essay/dissertation/article/conference paper the author is required to be familiar with, and provide a critical review of, the academic debate pertinent to the topic. This could involve explaining how the debate has developed over time and its current status, and identifying whether there is any consensus on the topic and, if not, what the different points of view are.

A literature review is more than a summary of previous work. It takes a critical stance, highlighting shortcomings, identifying gaps in the literature, asking questions that should be answered, and making a case for further investigation and research. It is usually written in past tense.

sentence starters

The current trend in this field centres on …

However, other studies have shown/revealed …

… provided some valuable insights into …

In contrast to previous studies …

There is a substantial body of literature on …

… summarised the view of most observers that …

‹author(s)› summarised the view of most observers that …

‹topic› has to date received quite detailed scholarly attention, with the bulk of these studies focusing on …

Much of the recent work in the area has concentrated on …

‹topic› has been a controversial and much disputed subject within the field of …

The causes of ‹topic› have been the subject of intense debate …

‹author(s)›, after examining arguments on both sides of the debate, concluded that …

To date there has been little agreement on …

The general consensus among scholars is that …

‹author(s)› published his/her/their controversial work in which …

This led to a disproportionate focus on …

Another/Other key idea(s) that emerge(s) from the literature is/are …

The commonly held view is that …

Absent from the literature is …

The study casts doubt upon the finding that …

useful vocabulary

absent	has again become	it demonstrates	the central focus of
after	however	language of the debate	the first of these
as soon as	in contrast to	reveals	the most recent
assumed	in the immediate aftermath	silent	then
even more	including	similarly	there is little doubt

example

Almost as soon as the guns opened fire in Europe in 1914, historians and commentators began seeking explanations for the causes of World War One, known at the time as the Great War. **There is a substantial body of literature on** the topic: it has been estimated that 30 000 books and scholarly articles have been written about the Great War. In the immediate aftermath of the war, **the general consensus amongst historians was that** Germany was solely responsible for starting the war. Then, in the 1920s and 1930s, post-war revisionist historians argued that it was unreasonable to blame Germany alone, and that Russia must bear some responsibility because of its mobilisation.

However, in 1961 Fischer **published his controversial work in which** he placed complete blame for the conflict on Germany. The Fischer thesis, as it became known, **provided valuable insights because** Fischer was the first historian to gain complete access to the WW1 German archives. In the late 1960s the British historian A. J. P. Taylor developed an even more specific argument relating to German guilt. **The central focus of his study** was that the sole cause of the war was the German adoption of the Schlieffen Plan. This military plan, with its complex detail and reliance on fastidiously planned railway timetables to move troops and equipment, meant, Taylor contended, that Germany became locked into declaring war on France. In the lead up to the centenary of the 1914–1918 conflict, the Great War has again become the centre of detailed scholarly attention, **with much of the recent work concentrating on** the argument that blame should be shared across all of the major belligerents in the conflict. There is little doubt that the debate over who started the war will continue well into the 21st century.

Citations for the many studies mentioned in this example would normally be included throughout.

summarising

purpose

briefly stating the main points in a short account, with details omitted

things to know

Summarising is a difficult skill. Note-making is an integral part of summarising and texts should be reduced to key points (in bullet point form) before attempting to write a summary.

Summaries are used in two ways:

- *to briefly restate what you have written earlier (citations are not required as they should have been provided when the issue was discussed in more detail); or*
- *to briefly outline what has been written elsewhere (citations are required).*

Like a conclusion, a summary of what you have written in your document NEVER introduces new information. That is why citations are not usually included.

sentence starters

So, to summarise the argument in this paper/section …

So, to restate the opening remarks, the key ideas are …

Stated another way, the essential idea is …

Generally, these key ideas emerge from the information/literature …

The reasons for … can be grouped into two categories: …

For the most part, …

A common observation in the literature is …

All evidence/supporting documentation points to …

All the evidence suggests …

The significant points that appear include …

… can be summarised in the following way(s): …

The essence of the argument is …

The essential ideas are summarised in the diagram below; namely, …

The main ideas related to the topic of … are …

The central idea presented in this text is …

This key idea forms the basis of …

The amount of detail given makes it easy to overlook the key idea, which is …

useful vocabulary

are as follows	hence	normally	then
at a glance	in a nutshell	often	thus
cases	in essence	on the whole	to begin with
crucially	in most/many	primarily	to conclude
essentially	in summary	second/secondly	together
finally	include(s)	states	
first/firstly	main/mainly	suggest/suggests	
generally	most importantly	sum up	

example

In summary, smoking damages people's health, increases their financial stress and erodes their quality of life, therefore understanding why some people are able to give up smoking more easily than others is vital. Almost two thirds of smokers want to give up their habit; however, they find it difficult to do so. Smokers, rather than being a hardened group, try many times to stop smoking, employing a variety of ways. Encouragingly, the enthusiasm for giving up is much higher than it was ten years ago. **For the most part**, smokers who try to give up without any support are less likely to succeed than those who seek help. Counselling and medication can double, sometimes triple, the rate of success. **Another key idea that emerges from the literature** is that different success rates are linked to socio-economic status. **Generally**, smokers with professional backgrounds show more desire and determination to stop smoking and have a greater success rate. **All the evidence suggests** that the proverb, "If at first you don't succeed, try, try, and try again", applies to giving up smoking – the more times smokers try to give up, the more likely they are to succeed. **This key idea forms the basis of** several current advertising campaigns.

synthesising information

purpose

putting together various elements (from several places or sources) to make a whole

things to know

Synthesising is an important and complex skill required in academic writing. Unlike summarising, which is condensing and restating the main ideas, synthesising involves combining, comparing and contrasting ideas from several sources, to see them in a new way and draw your own conclusions. The reassembled material is original.

Credibility of arguments is enhanced when many reliable and accurate sources are included.

sentence starters

Thus … can be said to …

Some researchers have commented on/observed …

Researchers are in general agreement that …

Previous studies/several studies have reported/identified …

Earlier studies questioned …

From these details, a conclusion can be drawn.

Clearly, it can be concluded that …

Recent evidence suggests that …

Studies of X emphasise the importance of …

Allowing for recent developments in the field, this work suggests …

A number of researchers have reported that …

Factors found to be influencing … have been explored in several studies that …

In the past two decades a number of researchers have sought to determine …

There have been a number of studies involving … that have reported …

Two contradictory points of view emerge from the evidence presented in several studies of …

It is surprising that this idea/solution/point of view has not been seriously considered before.

The information from … is in direct contradiction to the information from … in that …

Some commentators/researchers believe that …

Many claim …

The combined work and findings of … support the assertion/challenge the view that …

A comparison with the findings of earlier research makes it reasonable to propose …

The findings corroborate/contradict the earlier research that showed …

useful vocabulary

although	combines	in order for	so
as a result	consequently	in that respect	merge together
because	drawn together	include	therefore
blended the ideas	even though	instead of	whereas
but	exclude	joins/joined	while/whilst
cause/caused/causes	furthermore	nevertheless	
collectively	however	on the other hand	

example

Whilst there is no official or agreed upon definition of a global or world language, **researchers are in general agreement that** it is characterised by some common features*. A global language is the language learned and spoken internationally by a significant proportion of native and second-language speakers. It acts as a *lingua franca,* enabling people from diverse backgrounds to communicate in international arenas and diplomatic channels. **Several studies* have identified** reasons for that language to be English, including: its flexibility; its relative simplicity in terms of spelling, grammar and punctuation; the absence of coding for social and gender differences; and the richness and depth of the language's vocabulary. **Many claim** that English has already attained a place as the language of commerce, technology, education, tourism and sport*. **Earlier studies questioned** the unassailable position that English appears to be in as a contender for the status of the world language*. Those who have wielded the most power at any given time in history have seen their languages dominate (for example, Latin, French, and Spanish have all been universal languages at different times in the past). **The combined work and findings of ...* challenge the view** that English has this position. They do this by suggesting that, should the English-speaking nations of the world lose their dominance in the future, then it is highly likely that other countries, including China, may see one of their languages elevated to the status of a global or world language.

Citation(s) providing the source(s) of this information or evidence for these assertion(s) would normally be included here.

transitioning

purpose

assisting the reader to navigate a lengthy document

things to know

It is easier for readers to navigate a lengthy document if there are links between sections reminding the reader of what has gone before and foreshadowing what is coming next. This is called signposting. It can be particularly helpful for the reader if they are interrupted while reading the document, or if they choose to read some sections out of order (many markers read the first and last sections first, and then go back to look at the detail in the middle of the document).

The introductory section should end with a paragraph describing what is to come in the rest of the document. The information on writing introductions (pages 30 and 31) may assist in writing this. Additionally, each section needs an opening sentence that links it to the preceding section. At the end of each section, the final paragraph should provide a link to the next section. Finally, the last part of the concluding section should include a summary of the entire document.

Signposting sentences use past tense for earlier sections and present tense for the sections yet to come.

Allow for signposting sentences and paragraphs when planning the number of words to be written in a lengthy document.

sentence starters

This report/paper/thesis/article/study explores …

This report/paper/thesis/article/study has/contains/comprises … sections: …

The report/paper/thesis/article/study commenced with …

Following this introduction …

The previous section presented/discussed/explained/analysed …

This section continues the argument by …

This section, having described …, the next section presents/examines/details/explains …

This section analyses/discusses/examines … from three perspectives: …

There are three arguments for …

There are three aspects of … that are pertinent to this report/paper/thesis/article/study …

This idea is discussed in three parts: …

To summarise this section, …

The final section of …

The report/paper/thesis/article/study concluded that …

useful vocabulary

after	at the outset	in summary	prior to
also	at the same time	initially	so far
and then (use sparingly)	by	lastly	subsequently
as a final point	every time	meanwhile	the next section
as before	finally	moreover	this section
as soon as	first, second, third, etc.	now that	ultimately
as well as	following/followed	once	
at the beginning	formerly	previously	

example

At the end of the introduction: **This** experimental **report contains five sections.** Following this introduction, some background research is presented, leading to the development of six hypotheses about the rusting of steel. The second section on experimental process describes the experimental design, procedures, and method, and is followed by a third section that presents the observed data. In the discussion section, the data is analysed and deductions are made. The report ends with recommendations to prevent the corrosion of steel and a conclusion.

At the beginning of a section: **The previous section presented** the data collected in the experiment. **This section analyses and discusses** that data.

This section, having described *the procedure used to conduct the experiment,* **the next section presents** *the results of that experiment.*

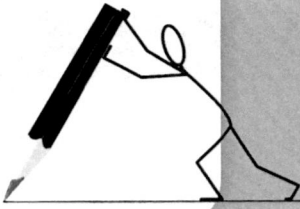

identifying the purposes of writing

This book provides reusable language, in the form of sentence starters and useful words, to demonstrate the many purposes of writing. Rarely does a piece of writing have a single purpose and academic writing, in particular, has many purposes. Extended written responses, in the form of assignments, research papers, articles and theses, have different parts that are written for different purposes. In lengthy documents each part is drafted separately and put together into one document before the extended piece of writing is finalised. The parts may not be written in the same order as they are presented in the final document.

If writing involves answering a question, recognising the purpose of writing is done by identifying the words in the question(s) that guide the writer towards the type of response required. Words such as *compare, analyse, justify, extrapolate*, and so on, give a clear idea of the skills required for that section of the writing. A comprehensive glossary of these words is provided on pages 67 to 70. However, sometimes the intent of the question is less obvious. For example, at first glance a question such as, 'Is X better than Y?' seems simple enough. In fact, the intent of the question is evaluation (weighing up the pros and cons of X and Y) and justification (making a decision and defending it).

Before commencing any writing, students should ensure that they are clear about the intent of the question. In other words, 'How does the examiner want me to respond to this question?' The table below shows a few examples of questions and intent.

If the question asks …,	then the intent is to …	so use the sentence starters and useful language of …
What are the parts of … and how are they related?	analyse	analysing
Give evidence and examples that support your explanation.	elaborate	elaborating
What are the characteristics of …?	describe	describing
State the idea in a more general way.	generalise	generalising
Defend your findings with relevant information.	justify	justifying

If the question asks …,	then the intent is to …	so use the sentence starters and useful language of …
Propose a solution to the problem of …	discuss and/or recommend	discussing recommending
In what ways are … similar and different?	compare	comparing
Give reasons for …	explain	explaining

If the writing involves a lengthy document with many parts, such as an experimental report or a thesis, the writer must determine which parts are required, and the purpose of each of them. The 24 purposes of writing explained in this book may assist in identifying which form of writing is appropriate in each part of the document.

writing to a word or page limit

Most assessment tasks have a word limit, for three reasons:

- It indicates the extent of the detail needed. Longer tasks indicate that points should be developed in more detail, not necessarily that there should be more points.

- Those marking your work do not have the time needed to read excessively long documents.

- Writing to length is an important skill. It ensures that you use your judgement to select the important information.

If your document is too long you may be penalised in the grading. The marker may stop reading after the required word length has been reached, so you will not receive credit for the information provided at the end of the document. Finally, some subjects (for example mathematics, sciences, business) value conciseness and may penalise you for sentence structures that use more words than necessary. If your document is too short, it is likely that it will not contain enough information, reducing the grade you might receive.

An A4 page typed using the Microsoft Word default font, margins and line spacing contains approximately 500 words. There is usually a 10% tolerance in word limits. That means if the limit is stated as 2000 words, then 2200 words will usually be accepted. Word limits do not usually include the text in the abstract, appendices, attachments, footnotes, endnotes or reference lists. However, you should check this with your tutor.

The following guidelines may be useful in planning your writing:

- The introduction should take about 10% of the word limit.

- The number of words devoted to each point will vary according to the amount of information available and the level of detail expected.

A reasonable guide for shorter tasks (those with a word count of fewer than 5000 words) is 150–300 words per point. Remember that longer tasks indicate that points should be developed in more detail (and hence more words), not necessarily that there should be more points.

- Allow space for the transitioning sentences and paragraphs (see pages 48 and 49).
- The conclusion should take about 10% to 15% of the word limit.

Academic writing can be published, for example, in journals, or as conference proceedings. In such cases, word limits may be replaced by page limits. You will often be told the size of margins, fonts and line spacing to use, or you may be required to use a pre-prepared downloadable template. Page limits may force you to rethink your use of tables, diagrams, lists and other presentations that can take up unnecessary space on the page.

In summary, when planning your writing, you should also plan how much you will write in each part in order to meet the stated word or page limit.

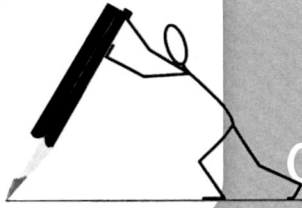

general principles of academic writing

Academic writing is used to communicate ideas in a formal and structured way. In most cases it is objective, although qualitative research can take account of the ontological position (world view) of the researcher and allow a more subjective approach.

structure

Scholarly documents usually follow a conventional structure. The detail of the structure may vary according to the purpose of the document.

A common structure for describing **academic research** is:
- introduction, describing the context, research question(s), and the direction of the study
- literature review, summarising and synthesising previous work on the topic
- methodology and methods, explaining how the information was collected and analysed
- results and discussion, describing the information collected and analysing what it means
- conclusion, summarising the study, explaining the key findings, and discussing the limitations of the study and the implications for future research
- references, listing the sources of information used in the document.

Essays are usually structured with:
- an introduction, describing what the essay is about and the direction that it will take
- a body, discussing the main ideas, including explanations and/or evidence from scholarly readings and from your own work, examples, and your critical evaluation and synthesis of these ideas
- a conclusion, summarising and evaluating the main ideas and commenting on the significance of the topic
- references, listing the sources of information used in the document.

The structure of **experimental reports** includes:
- posing the question
- undertaking background research in order to make predictions
- developing one or more hypotheses based on those predictions
- testing the hypothesis by experimentation
- analysing the experimental results, including any limitations of the data
- drawing conclusions and recommending (if appropriate)
- references, listing the sources of information used in the document.

If the document is lengthy, the structure can be made clear to the reader (signposted) by the use of section headings.

language choices

Brevity requires that your language choices be precise and concise, avoiding unnecessary words. However, some faculties discourage the excessive use of point form (that is, the presentation in this section). Other features to consider include:

> **George Orwell's rules for clear writing**
>
> 1. Never use a metaphor, simile, or other figure of speech that you are used to seeing in print.
> 2. Never use a long word when a short one will do.
> 3. If it is possible to cut a word out, always cut it out.
> 4. Never use the passive when you can use the active.
> 5. Never use a foreign phrase, a scientific word, or a jargon word if you can think of an everyday English equivalent.
> 6. Break any of these rules sooner than say anything barbarous.

- Be professional – use a formal tone, usually written in the third person.
- Do not confuse written language with speech – for example, most sentences will still make sense if these words are not used: absolutely, actually, amazing, apparently, basically, honestly, just, literally, obviously, quite, really, stuff, very.
- Vary your sentence length, using a mixture of short, medium, and long sentences – 20 to 25 words is a good average target; if you find your sentence is as long as a paragraph, go back to investigate ways of splitting the sentence into two or more shorter sentences.
- Use adjectives sparingly – many of them are opinions, not fact – for example, *significant, substantial, insubstantial, considerable, inappropriate, appropriate, excessive, limited*.
- Do not use double negatives – for example, *the evidence is certainly not irrefutable* is better written as *the evidence can be refuted*.
- Avoid contractions (for example, *can't*) and clichés (for example *reading between the lines*).
- Express ideas positively – for example, what should be done rather than what should not be done.
- Use the active rather than the passive voice where possible; passive voice is acceptable when you want to emphasise the object or recipient of the action rather than the agent of the action.
- Use inclusive, non-discriminatory language, avoiding gender-specific pronouns; do not refer to gender, religion, sexual orientation, nationality, racial group, age and physical or mental characteristics unless they are critical to the meaning of the text.

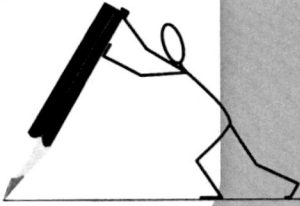

presentation – formats, styles and page layouts

The presentation of documents is important in academic writing. Authors can be required to use particular document formats. Almost all academic journals specify the format of the manuscript submitted for publication and provide templates for prospective authors to use. Some faculties have preferred formats and may specify and/or produce publication manuals or templates for student use.

There are some excellent publication manuals that provide details about writing styles and formats, often linked to subject areas. For example, the *Publication Manual of the American Psychological Association* is commonly used in the social sciences, including education. The publication manuals should be available in your university library and many summaries of them are available online. If the general guidelines listed below are insufficient or conflict with advice from your faculty, refer to the publication manual recommended by your faculty.

margins and line spacing

White space on the page, created by suitable paragraphing, margins and blank lines, not only looks better, but can make it easier for the reader.

Where possible, aim for paragraphs of 200 words or fewer. Allow extra space between paragraphs.

A 2.5 cm margin all round works well on A4 paper. If you plan to bind your document, the margin on the inside of the page should be wider to accommodate the binding. Some markers prefer to have a wider margin on the right side of the page to allow them to make annotations or attach electronic comments.

Single line spacing can look cramped – line spacing between 1.08 and 1.15 points is easier to read. In some academic documents one-and-a-half or double line spacing is required. The script or speaking notes for a spoken presentation can be easier to follow if the lines are double-spaced.

fonts and text styles

Standard fonts, for example, Times New Roman, Arial or Calibri, in 11 or 12 point, are preferred as they are easy to read. The same font style should be used consistently throughout a document. However, the text in titles, headings, table and figure captions, blocked quotations, footnotes, labels in tables and figures, and reference lists may use different sizes and boldface and/or italic versions of the font.

Italics can be used (a) for emphasis, (b) for a word or phrase used as an example (such as, 'The difference between *lesser* and *fewer* is …'), (c) to introduce a technical term, or (d) for the title of a work. Boldface type is generally used only in headings. Underlining is reserved for URLs (web addresses). Besides for direct quotations, double quotation marks are used when changing the meaning of a word (e.g. 'It is considered "normal" behaviour'), but only the first time the word or phrase is used in that sense.

Unexplained changes of font styles and sizes, and of line spacing, can indicate that the affected text has been cut from another source and pasted into the document with little amendment. Markers are experienced in spotting these types of oversights.

Resist the temptation to overcome page limits by using a smaller font or compressed character spacing – university teachers are used to writing to word and page limits themselves and know all the tricks, probably better than students. Writing extra text in small, white coloured font to pad out the word length shown in the footer of an electronic document is also a ploy well-known to markers.

Keep text formatting simple …

- *no italics*
- **no boldface**
- <u>no underlined words</u>
- <u>no words underlined twice</u>
- no marks of overexcitement!!!!!
- no UAs
- (no ideas added in parentheses)
- no "quotation marks" without good reason
- no Random Capitalisation
- NO SHOUTING
- no changes **in** font

    … without a good reason.

(by the way, UA means unexplained abbreviations)

headers, footers and page numbering

Headers and footers are often used to contain information about the document, for example the title, chapter name, and page numbers. Section breaks between the main sections of a document enable the use of different footers for each section (such as the chapter name in each chapter). The second and subsequent pages of any document should be numbered, usually in the footer. Longer documents such as theses (and this book) often use Roman numerals for the page numbering of preliminary pages and Arabic numerals for the remainder of the document, restarting at number 1 for the first page of the main document and continuing through to the end of the document, including references and appendices.

footnotes and endnotes

Footnotes (at the bottom of the page) or endnotes (at the end of the document or chapter) can be used to provide supplementary information. As they can be distracting to the reader, they should be used sparingly. Some publications do not permit the use of footnotes or endnotes. If the contents of a footnote or endnote cannot be woven in to the body of the text, you should question whether they are essential to the argument.

citations and references

References give the source of quotations and other information used in an academic document (for example, books, journals and websites) and are listed in detail at the end of the document. References are an important way of providing evidence. A citation is a code embedded in the text of the document, usually in brackets, for example (Smith, 2014) or [24]. It links to a source listed in the reference section. In the case of a direct quote from a source, the citation includes the page number(s).

Many different styles of citations and references are available. Most faculties have a preferred citation/reference style as each discipline tends to use only one or two styles. If in doubt, students should check with their faculty or tutor about the preferred style. While the style of citations and references can vary, all references usually include: author(s); date; title; and publication details.

Software is available to manage citations and references, for example, EndNote and BibTex. Universities often have a software licence that allows their students to freely download and use such software, and provide training in their use. This software is highly recommended to ensure accuracy and completeness in referencing.

taking notes

The first stage in academic writing is taking notes about information in the source documents you have located. The source documents can include academic journal articles, books and conference papers. While it is generally safest to rely on sources that provide their own references (pointing the way to more source documents for your research) and are peer-reviewed, blogs and newspaper reports can provide useful information about recent events and opinion (it can take up to two years for research to be documented, peer-reviewed and published).

Confine your note taking to what is relevant to the topic you are researching. Make any handwritten notes on one side of the page only, so you can spread all your notes out on a table later. You are the only audience for your notes, so you can use any abbreviations, symbols and shorthand that you choose. The only requirement is that you can understand your own notes later.

Many recent publications are available in electronic form. If you are using a computer to make notes from electronic source documents, it can be tempting to cut and paste into your own notes. However, you must have a system of recording if the passage of text is a direct copy so that you do not inadvertently plagiarise it later. Colouring all copied text in red is one way of keeping track of which parts of your notes are in your words and which parts are not. Keep a record of the page number of any sections of text you might want to include as a direct quotation in your paper.

Initially, structure your notes according to their source. It is important to record the details of the source document for later inclusion in the references section of your paper. The use of bibliographic software such as EndNote or BibTex can save time, and is worth the initial effort required to input the data in a way that will be useful later. If you have an electronic copy of the source document, save it for later reference. Electronic documents should be given meaningful names (because the titles of some papers can be lengthy, use the combination of the primary author's family name and the year of publication as the file name) and sorted into suitably named folders so they can be located easily later. Regular back-up of computer records is essential, as the loss of this information will not be accepted as a reason for not meeting submission deadlines.

As you continue to read, the important themes of the topic should start to emerge. When you think you have enough information to fully cover the topic and to meet the prescribed word limit, use a mind map (concept map) to develop a thematic plan for the final structure of your paper.

Restructure your notes to fit your thematic plan. One way of doing this is to cut up a copy of your notes into separate ideas and shuffle them about on a large table into the themes. Other ways are to colour code (using a highlighter) or label (code) each idea thematically. If your notes are on computer, they can be restructured into themes using the cut and paste functions. Ensure you keep your original copy of your notes so that you can still find the source of each idea.

You are now ready to start drafting your paper. Use the information in the various sections of this book to assist. Remember to paraphrase any sections that you copied directly from the source documents (which you coloured red) or to present them in your paper as direct quotes, suitably acknowledged with citations.

writing abstracts

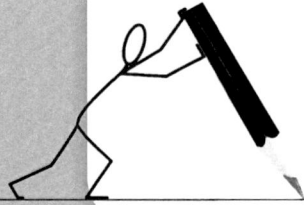

A lengthy report or article will require an abstract. An abstract is a concise summary of what the report or article is about and is usually placed before the body of your writing. It can be read to get an overview. It tells the reader what to expect in your work and should be based on all you have written.

Abstracts are the first thing people read when they want to know what you have written about. They are your opportunity to advertise your work. Most library database search engines display the abstract in the results, but not the full text of the work. This allows the reader to decide whether to download a full copy. Similarly, in a conference, the abstract of a presentation will be printed in the conference program, allowing the participants to decide if they want to attend the session. In a thesis for a higher degree, the abstract may be published in the program for the graduation ceremony.

A good abstract uses a single coherent and concise paragraph. It should make sense to a person who has not read the paper. It covers all the essential elements of the whole paper, for example, what you did, why you did it, how you did it, what you found out, and why it was important. It should not use information that is not included in the paper.

The abstract is the last part of the writing process. To write an abstract, read your paper to refresh your memory about its contents. Then read each section and summarise the information in one or two short sentences. When all sentences are written, read them again to ensure that they cover the major points in your paper. Check the word length prescribed for the abstract (this can vary, but is usually from 100 to 250 words) and further reduce the number of words, if necessary, by removing unnecessary words or rewriting some of the sentences into a single, more succinct sentence. Check that the abstract does not contain any unexplained abbreviations. Finally, edit the abstract to ensure that it flows and is not repetitive in content or vocabulary.

using numbers

When presenting numerical information, there is a choice between using symbols (numbers) and words. The advice below is taken from the *Publication Manual of the American Psychological Association*, which applies to writing in sociology, education and psychology. For more detail, including exceptions and special usages, refer to the recommended publication manual for your faculty or discipline.

To assist the reader, numbers with five or more digits use spaces (not commas) to group the digits in threes. For example, 23 456, not 23,456 or 23456.

Use numbers (symbols) for:

- numbers with two or more digits (i.e. 10 and above, and all decimals and fractions)
- dates, ages, time and money
- the number of people in a study
- grade or year level (e.g. at school)
- page and chapter numbering
- scales or ratings (e.g. '3 out of 45 people')
- numbers used in comparison with other numbers with two or more digits (e.g. 'of the 16 students surveyed, 3 said that ..., 6 responded ...').

Use words for:

- single digit numbers (i.e. 0, 1, 2, ..., 9)
- numbers that begin a title
- numbers that begin a sentence (restructure the sentence to avoid beginning with a number, if possible: e.g. 'Fifteen of the respondents to the survey said that ...')
- numbers in a hyphenated word (e.g. 'He was a ten-time winner').

When using several numbers, list them from largest to smallest (e.g. 'The group included 10 people who were born in Australia, 3 born in the United Kingdom and 1 born in New Zealand'). If a total is involved, report the total before the categories (e.g. 'The group of 14 people included 10 people who were born in Australia, 3 born in the United Kingdom and 1 born in New Zealand').

using tense

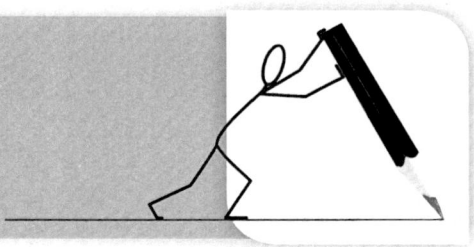

Managing tense can be tricky. Consistency is important. If you use past tense at the start of a sentence or paragraph, you should use past tense throughout.

Some guidelines about the use of tense in academic writing are listed below.

Use present tense (*it is*) for:

- events that apply currently (e.g. 'The Prime Minister of Australia is ...')
- describing a theory with continuing applicability (e.g. 'Darwin's theory of natural selection states that ...')
- discussing the implications of your results
- presenting your conclusions
- referring to parts of the current document that are yet to come (e.g. 'This section reports the results of the experiment, while the next section shows that ...').

Use past tense (*it was*) for:

- actions that occurred at a definite time in the past (e.g. 'President John Kennedy died in 1963')
- reporting experimental results
- referring to previous parts of the current document (e.g. 'The introduction explained that ...')
- writing an abstract (other than any conclusions with continuing applicability)
- discussing another document (since it was written in the past).

Use present perfect tense (*it has been*) for:

- a past action that did not occur at a specific time (e.g. 'Researchers have shown that ...')
- an action that commenced in the past and continues into the future (e.g. 'Since then, several researchers have used that method.').

degrees of intensity (modality)

MODE	LOW						HIGH
probability	impossible/impossibly	improbable/improbably	unlikely	possible/possibly	likely/in all likelihood	probable/probably	sure/surely	certain/certainly
frequency	never	seldom	occasional/occasionally	sometimes	often	usual/usually	regularly/in most cases	always
certainty	never	scarce/scarcely	perhaps/in some cases	might/could	as likely as not	inevitable/inevitably	undoubted/undoubtedly	definite/definitely
extent	never	scarce/scarcely	limited	partly	general/generally	mainly	mostly	complete/completely
confidence	suspect	unreasonable/unreasonably	doubtful/doubtfully	moderate/moderately	reasonable/reasonably	plausible/plausibly	undeniable/undeniably	irrefutable/irrefutably
importance	desirable/desirably	prefer/preferably	require/required	necessary	important/importantly	essential/essentially	unquestionable/unquestionably	vital/vitally
intensity	scarce/scarcely	slight/slightly	mild/mildly	intermittent/intermittently	moderate/moderately	typical/typically	unrelenting/unrelentingly	extreme/extremely

Caution: The adjectives and adverbs in this table are often used to convey an opinion. If they are used in academic writing, the choice of word would usually be supported by evidence.

alternatives to 'said'

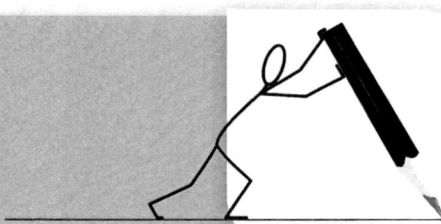

explanation

It is common practice in academic writing to relate what other people have said or written. To repeatedly use the word 'said' can be tedious and unsophisticated. The list below provides some alternatives.

acknowledged	made it clear
admitted	noted
agreed	offered a well-considered solution
alleged	offered an alternative explanation
announced	opined
argued	pleaded the case for
asserted	proposed
came to the conclusion	put forward the view
claimed	refuted
clarified	rejected
commented	reported the findings
concluded	repudiated the arguments
contradicted the commonly held beliefs	resolved
contended	revealed
declared	showed
demonstrated	stated
denied	stressed
described	suggested
emphasised	supported the argument that
estimated	told
explained	urged the reader to
found	vehemently denied
indicated	

first person or third person?

explanation

In most forms of formal, academic writing, the use of the first person (*I, me, my* or, if the text is a collaborative effort, *we, us, our*) is generally discouraged. Excessive use of the first person can result in texts that focus more on the writer than the subject at hand. A text can have more academic rigour, authority or greater objectivity if it is written in the third person. In addition, the use of the passive voice (i.e. the 'doer' is removed) is a prominent feature of many technical texts. However, attempts to avoid the use of first person can lead to lengthy and confusing sentences.

In recent decades, there has been increasing acceptance of academic writing in the first person. The use of first person may suit the form of writing. In some cases, omitting personal references can result in fewer compelling statements, and may appear to be indecisive. In some forms of writing the author may be expected to describe their background or personal learning journey, or to give an opinion. Attempting to do this in third person sounds unnatural.

However, your faculty may have its own guidelines about the use of first person. It is sometimes a hot topic, and opinions vary. If in doubt, check with your tutor.

If you decide to write in third person, the phrases below provide some ways to avoid the use of the first person.

It could be suggested that …

This is/can be illustrated by …

It is seen through …

This is evident when …

Upon examination, it was apparent that …

The facts indicate that …

This is exemplified by …

This illustrates that …

This shows that …

Therefore, it can be stated that …

This becomes apparent when …

With some exceptions, sources generally agree that …

… clearly points out that …

This is most obvious when …

It can, therefore, be observed that …

There is evidence to support both opinions on this topic.

‹Author 1› (‹date›) agrees/disagrees with ‹author 2› (‹date›) about …

The most notable exceptions to this rule are …

Observations reveal that …

key task word glossary

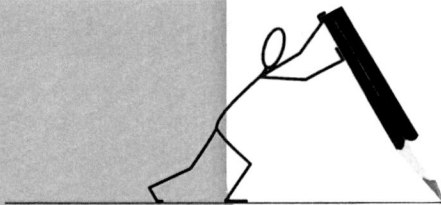

abstract	to create a general idea about something rather than one relating to a particular object, person or situation
account for	to give reasons for something and report on those reasons
account for (maths)	to report on; to try every possibility
analyse	to examine the parts of something in detail and discuss or interpret the relationship of the parts to each other and to the whole; may involve description, comparison, explanation, interpretation and critical comment
analyse (maths)	to use statistical methods to summarise, compare or infer something
appraise	to consider something or someone carefully and form an opinion about it or them
argue	to present one or both sides of an argument or case to reach a conclusion; arguing may involve the use of persuasive techniques (these are factual and logical rather than emotive) to convince others that your opinion about something is the correct one
arrange	to place things into a particular position, often with a degree of order or precision
assess	to make a judgement about something based on its value or worth (may include quality, outcomes, results or size)
assume	to accept that something is true without necessarily confirming it or checking its validity
calculate	to ascertain or determine something from facts, figures or information
calculate (maths)	to obtain a result from given facts, data or other numeric information about something
categorise	to divide things or people into sets or say to which set they belong based on common criteria
classify	to group things with similarities in the same classes or categories; to defend the inclusion of similar things into these categories
comment on	to present your opinion about something
compare	to identify the ways in which two or more things are similar and different
conclude	to draw together the main ideas of something and restate them in a succinct way, often as a decision
consider	to give opinions in relation to the information you have been given about something or someone

consider (maths)	to ensure that your response refers to the particular information you have been given about something
construct	to make, build or put together items or arguments about something
contrast	to examine two or more things and focus on the differences
criticise	to make judgements about something or someone, giving details to support your views
decide	to choose something or someone based on a consideration of other possibilities
debate	to examine both sides of an issue about something and come to a conclusion – or leave the reader/listener the opportunity to come to a conclusion
deduce	to reach a conclusion about something based on evidence that is known to be true
defend	to argue in support of something
define	to show, describe or state clearly what something is and what its limits are
define (maths)	to give the meaning or precise description of the concept
demonstrate	to show something by example
describe	to give a detailed account of the properties, qualities, features or parts of something or someone
devise	to have an idea for something and design and plan it
differentiate	to recognise or show the differences between one thing or person and another
differentiate (maths)	to find a derivative
discriminate	to recognise that two things or people are different
distinguish	to draw attention to, and make note of, the distinct differences between things or people
discuss	to consider the results of research and the implications of those results; to consider both sides of an issue about something, without necessarily coming to a conclusion
elaborate	to give more information or detail about something
evaluate	to consider something or someone to make a judgement of value or worth; often supported by evidence
evaluate (maths)	to find the exact value of something
examine	to look at something carefully, often for reasons 'how' or 'why' something may have happened
exemplify	to give more information or details about something

key task word glossary

explain	to make the reader understand something by giving a detailed account of its properties, qualities, features or parts, how it works, and why it is as it is
expound	to present a clear and convincing argument for a definite and detailed opinion about something
extend	to include or affect other people or things
extract	to obtain information from a larger amount or source of information
extrapolate	to use known facts about something as a basis for general statements about a situation or what is likely to happen in the future
extrapolate (maths)	to extend a graph to obtain additional values
generalise	to develop a broad statement that seems to be true in most situations or for most people; this does not include details such as data, quotations, or examples
generalise (maths)	to use particular examples of something to develop an equation or mathematical model to describe the overall situation
identify	to notice or discover the existence or presence of something or someone
illustrate	to use examples of something to give more detail to information or more weight to an argument
indicate	to point out something from available information
infer	to use what is provided to make meaning or arrive at an answer; to uncover the answer even though it is not directly said or stated
interpret	to examine a piece of text and explain its meaning or significance, often from a particular point of view
introduce	to start a text by describing what it is about
investigate	to examine the reasons for something
justify	to show or prove that a decision, action or idea about something is reasonable or necessary by giving sound, plausible and logical reasons for it; answers the question 'why'
justify (maths)	to give all the logical reasons and/or mathematical arguments that have led to a decision
list	to arrange related items in order, usually under one another (i.e. vertically)
order	to arrange things in a logical way
outline	to give all the main ideas about something without the details
paraphrase	to restate what someone has said or written in a slightly different way from the way it was first stated; the meaning is retained
predict	to suggest what might happen based on the available information

prepare	to gather what you need to make ready for something that is going to happen
present	to put forward something for consideration
propose	to put forward something (e.g. a plan, an idea, a point of view, an argument, a suggestion)
prove	to support something with facts and figures
prove (maths)	to produce a logical mathematical argument that shows the truth of a statement for all values or situations
quote	to repeat the exact words of the author (direct quotations) as evidence in writing
recommend	to suggest a course of action for consideration by others; to provide reasons (usually the findings of research or investigation) in favour of the suggestion
refer	to use material in your answer (without necessarily directly quoting) from the stimulus material or information
reflect	to respond in a personal way to experiences, situations, events or new information by making personal connections with the new material
review	to examine, describe, summarise, evaluate and clarify academic literature
sequence	to put things in the order in which things are arranged, actions are carried out, or events happen
sketch	to give the main ideas briefly about something or to create a sketch or drawing that shows the essential features; detail or accuracy is not required
solve	to find an answer or solution to a problem
suggest	to put forward or propose an idea or plan about something for someone to think about
support	to use a fact to support a statement or theory about something
summarise	to briefly state the main points in a short account with details omitted
synthesise	to put together various elements (from several places or sources) to make a whole; the reassembled material is original
trace	to show how events/arguments progress and develop
value	to establish the worth of something or someone
verify	to back up a particular result and prove something
verify (maths)	to test the truth of something

glossary

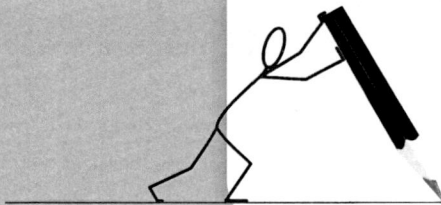

active voice	One of the two 'voices' of verbs (see also *passive voice*). In active voice, the subject of the sentence is doing the acting, as in the example *Tracy wrote the letter*. Tracy (the subject of the sentence) acts in relation to the letter.
audience	The intended readers of a document.
bibliography	A list of sources, such as books, articles, and websites, consulted in the process of preparing a document. The difference between a bibliography and a reference list is that the bibliography may contain sources that are not cited in the document. They were used in the pre-internet days to direct the reader to possible areas of further reading, but are less common now that internet-based searches are available.
brevity	The quality of expressing many ideas in few words.
citation	An alphanumeric code embedded in the text of a scholarly document, usually in brackets. A citation links to a source document listed in the reference section. As there are many different styles of citations used in academic disciplines, students should check with their teacher about the preferred citation style.
cliché	A commonly used expression; a sentence or phrase that may have once been apt or amusing, but has lost originality, ingenuity, and impact by overuse.
communication	The exchange of thoughts, opinions, or information by speech, writing, or signs.
concise	Providing information clearly, but with a minimum of words.
document	A written work, such as a book, article, letter, or report. If the document is stored on a computer, it may refer to the data file containing the written work.
e.g.	An abbreviation for *exempli gratia* (Latin), meaning *for example*.
epistemology	The study or theory of knowledge: what constitutes valid knowledge and how we obtain it.
et al.	An abbreviation for *et alia* (Latin), meaning, *and others*. It is used extensively in some citations.
etc.	An abbreviation for *et cetera* (Latin), meaning *and so on*.
formal language	Formal language is used when writing for serious, professional or academic purposes. It involves the precise use of vocabulary and grammar and an impersonal, polite tone. For example, formal language does not use colloquialisms or contractions, and tends to minimise use of first person pronouns such as 'I' or 'we'.

genre	A kind, category, or sort, especially of literary or artistic work.
i.e.	An abbreviation for *id est* (Latin), meaning *that is* or *in other words*.
inclusive language	Language that does not, directly or indirectly, exclude a section of the community.
literature review	A critical summary of previous scholarly work, highlighting shortcomings, identifying gaps in the research, asking questions that should be answered, and making a case for further investigation and research.
ontology	The study of what constitutes reality and how we understand existence. For example, a positivist ontology is concerned with objective (factual) knowledge based on a deductive or theory-testing approach in order to explain the world. On the other hand, an interpretivist ontology accommodates different perspectives and uses an inductive or theory-building approach to understand the world.
quote/quotation	The exact words of an author, or a person being studied.
passive voice	One of the two 'voices' of verbs (see also *active voice*). In passive voice, the subject of the sentence is acted on by the verb. For example, in *the article was written*, the subject (*the article*) receives the action of the verb (*was written*), and the agent or 'doer' of the action is omitted.
peer reviewed	The process of subjecting a scholarly work, research, or ideas to the scrutiny of others who are experts in the same field (peers), before it is published. Also known as refereeing.
purpose for writing	The reason for preparing a written document and the many different ways of writing within an extended written text, such as writing to explain, to justify, to evaluate, and so on. The 24 double-page sections that make up the first part of this book are all purposes for writing.
references	Sources such as books, websites, and personal communications used to obtain information contained in a document. References are an important way of providing evidence. While the format, or style, of the reference information can vary, all references usually include the following information: author(s); date; title; and publication details.
scholarly	Relating to serious, formal academic study or research.
signpost	To show the way to something. In a document, signposts provide cues and directions to readers to help them understand and navigate the document.
signposting	Headings or statements used in a written document to indicate what is to follow.
text	The contents of a written or printed work. It may include prose (words), symbols, tables, and/or visual images.
viz.	An abbreviation for *videlicet* (Latin), meaning *namely*.
writing style	The manner in which an author chooses to write to his or her readers. The writing style is influenced by the purpose for writing, the readers for whom the writing is intended and the writer's personality and voice.

my notes

my notes

about the authors

Patricia Hipwell M.Ed., B.Sc. Econ. (Hons), Grad. Dip. of Literacy Ed., P.G.C.E. is an independent literacy consultant for her own company, **logonliteracy**. She delivers literacy professional development to teachers in Australia, and works predominantly in Queensland schools. Patricia has specialised in assisting all teachers to be literacy teachers, especially high school subject specialists who often struggle with what it means to be a content area teacher and a literacy teacher.

Merilyn (Lyn) Carter Ph.D., M.Ed.(Research), Dip.Ed., B.Ec., operating through her business **Count on Numeracy,** is an independent consultant, providing professional development to teachers of numeracy and mathematics throughout Australia. She completed her doctoral thesis on NAPLAN numeracy testing. Lyn also works as a researcher at the Queensland University of Technology (QUT).

Patricia and Lyn have created a number of resources to assist students' literacy and numeracy development. Both consultants are available (as a cross-curricular team or individually) to provide professional development in their areas of expertise and to support the use of their recommended resources, including this one.

For further information, contact:

Patricia Hipwell
Mobile: 0429 727 313
email: pat.hipwell@gmail.com

logonliteracy

Merilyn (Lyn) Carter
Mobile: 0402 077 958
email: countonnumeracy@bigpond.com

Count on **Numeracy**